Study Guide & Working Papers

for

College Accounting

CHAPTERS 1-13

Fourteenth Edition

John Ellis Price
University of North Texas

M. David Haddock, Jr.
Chattanooga State Community College
Emeritus

Michael J. Farina
Cerritos College

Mc
Graw
Hill
Education

STUDY GUIDE & WORKING PAPERS FOR
COLLEGE ACCOUNTING: CHAPTERS 1-13, FOURTEENTH EDITION

Published by McGraw-Hill Education, 2 Penn Plaza, New York, NY 10121. Copyright © 2015 by McGraw-Hill Education. All rights reserved. Printed in the United States of America. Previous editions © 2012, 2009, 2007, 2003, 1999, 1996, 1994, 1990, 1986, 1981, 1974, 1969 and 1966. No part of this publication may be reproduced or distributed in any form or by any means, or stored in a database or retrieval system, without the prior written consent of McGraw-Hill Education, including, but not limited to, in any network or other electronic storage or transmission, or broadcast for distance learning.

Some ancillaries, including electronic and print components, may not be available to customers outside the United States.

This book is printed on acid-free paper.

3 4 5 6 7 8 9 0 ROV/ROV 1 0 9 8 7 6 5

ISBN: 978-0-07-763988-4
MHID: 0-07-763988-X

www.mhhe.com

Table of Contents

CHAPTER 1

Accounting: The Language of Business

STUDY GUIDE

Understanding the Chapter

Objectives

1. Define accounting. **2.** Identify and discuss career opportunities in accounting. **3.** Identify the users of financial information. **4.** Compare and contrast the three types of business entities. **5.** Describe the process used to develop generally accepted accounting principles. **6.** Define the accounting terms new to this chapter.

Reading Assignment

Read Chapter 1 in the textbook. Complete the textbook Section Self Review as you finish reading each section of the chapter, and the Comprehensive Self Review at the end of the chapter. Refer to the Chapter 1 Glossary or to the Glossary at the end of the book to find definitions for terms that are not familiar to you.

Activities

❏ **Thinking Critically**

Answer the *Thinking Critically* questions for Google and Managerial Implications.

❏ **Discussion Questions**

Answer each assigned discussion question in Chapter 1.

❏ **Critical Thinking Problem**

Complete the critical thinking problem as assigned.

❏ **Business Connections**

Complete the Business Connections activities as assigned to gain a deeper understanding of Chapter 1 concepts.

Practice Tests

Complete the Practice Tests, which cover the main points in your reading assignment. Compare your answers with those in the Practice Test Answer Key for Chapter 1 at the end of this chapter. If you have answered any questions incorrectly, review the related section of the text.

Part A True-False *For each of the following statements, circle T in the answer column if the answer is true or F if the answer is false.*

T F **1.** Because of the difference in the structures of the three types of business entities, certain aspects of their financial affairs are accounted for in different ways.

T F **2.** A sole proprietorship is a form of business entity owned by two or more people.

T F **3.** There is little difference between a corporation and other forms of business entities.

T F **4.** Shares of stock represent ownership in a corporation.

T F **5.** Employees should have no particular interest in the financial information about the business for which they work.

T F **6.** The American Institute of Certified Public Accountants is a governmental agency.

T F **7.** In a large company, the auditing process is completed by bookkeepers.

T F **8.** Passing a test called the Uniform CPA Examination is required for one to become a certified public accountant.

T F **9.** The Securities and Exchange Commission has a great deal of power to dictate accounting methods used by companies whose stock is traded on the stock exchanges.

T F **10.** The Securities and Exchange Commission often relies on pronouncements of the Financial Accounting Standards Board.

T F **11.** The Financial Accounting Standards Board issues income tax rules.

T F **12.** Because of the separate entity assumption, the personal financial activities of the owner of a sole proprietorship are combined with the financial affairs of his or her business in the accounting records of the business.

T F **13.** All accounting principles are established by law.

Part B Completion   *In the answer column, supply the missing word or words needed to complete each of the following statements.*

_____ 1. Many people call accounting the _____ _____ _____.

_____ 2. _____ _____ is the study of accounting principles used by different countries.

_____ 3. The IRS and the _____ have large numbers of accountants on their staff and use them to uncover possible violations of the law.

_____ 4. Major areas of accounting are public accounting, managerial accounting, and _____ _____.

_____ 5. The _____ is an organization of accounting educators.

_____ 6. The _____ is a national association of professional accountants.

_____ 7. _____ _____ _____ _____ are developed by the Financial Accounting Standards Board.

_____ 8. The _____ was created to review and oversee the accounting methods of publicly owned corporations.

_____ 9. The _____ and other tax authorities are interested in financial information about a firm.

_____ 10. Corporate owners are called _____ _____.

_____ 11. Ownership in a corporation is evidenced by _____ _____ _____.

_____ 12. The three major types of business entities are sole proprietorships, corporations, and _____.

_____ 13. An economic entity is an organization whose major purpose is to produce a profit, whereas a(n) _____ _____ is a nonprofit organization.

_____ 14. The accounting process involves _____, _____, summarizing, interpreting, and communicating financial information about an economic or social entity.

_____ 15. Periodic reports prepared from accounting records are called _____ _____.

WORKING PAPERS
CRITICAL THINKING PROBLEM 1.1

Name _____

_____

_____

_____

_____

_____

_____

_____

_____

_____

_____

_____

_____

_____

_____

_____

_____

_____

_____

_____

_____

_____

Chapter 1 Practice Test Answer Key

Part A True-False	Part B Completion
1. T	1. language of business
2. F	2. International accounting
3. F	3. FBI
4. T	4. governmental accounting
5. F	5. AAA
6. F	6. AICPA
7. F	7. Generally accepted accounting principles
8. T	8. SEC
9. T	9. IRS
10. T	10. stockholders or shareholders
11. F	11. shares of stock
12. F	12. partnerships
13. F	13. social entity
	14. recording, classifying
	15. financial statements

CHAPTER 2

Analyzing Business Transactions

STUDY GUIDE

Understanding the Chapter

Objectives	**1.** Record in equation form the financial effects of a business transaction. **2.** Define, identify, and understand the relationship between asset, liability, and owner's equity accounts. **3.** Analyze the effects of business transactions on a firm's assets, liabilities, and owner's equity and record these effects in accounting equation form. **4.** Prepare an income statement. **5.** Prepare a statement of owner's equity and a balance sheet **6.** Define the accounting terms new to this chapter.
Reading Assignment	Read Chapter 2 in the textbook. Complete the textbook Section Self Review as you finish reading each section of the chapter, and the Comprehensive Self Review at the end of the chapter. Refer to the Chapter 2 Glossary or to the Glossary at the end of the book to find definitions for terms that are not familiar to you.

Activities

❑ **Thinking Critically**	Answer the *Thinking Critically* questions for Southwest Airlines and Managerial Implications.
❑ **Discussion Questions**	Answer each assigned discussion question in Chapter 2.
❑ **Exercises**	Complete each assigned exercise in Chapter 2. Use the forms provided in this SGWP. The objectives covered by an exercise are given after the exercise number. If you need help with an exercise, review the portion of the chapter related to the objective(s) covered.
❑ **Problems A/B**	Complete each assigned problem in Chapter 2. Use the forms provided in this SGWP. The objectives covered by a problem are given after the problem number. If you need help with a problem, review the portion of the chapter related to the objective(s) covered.
❑ **Critical Thinking Problems 2.1 and 2.2**	Complete Critical Thinking Problems 2.1 and 2.2 as assigned. Use the forms provided in this SGWP.
❑ **Business Connections**	Complete the Business Connections activities as assigned to gain a deeper understanding of Chapter 2 concepts.

Practice Tests

	Complete the Practice Tests, which cover the main points in your reading assignment. Compare your answers with those in the Practice Test Answer Key for Chapter 2 at the end of this chapter. If you have answered any questions incorrectly, review the related section of the text.

Part A True-False   *For each of the following statements, circle T in the answer column if the answer is true or F if the answer is false.*

T   F   **1.** The balance sheet shows the financial position of a business on a specific date.

T   F   **2.** A profit and loss statement is another name for the income statement.

T   F   **3.** The balance sheet is prepared at the end of the accounting period to show the results of operations.

T   F   **4.** A net loss results if total expenses exceed total revenue.

T   F   **5.** The net income or net loss for the period is shown in the Assets section of the balance sheet.

T   F   **6.** The net income or net loss for the period is shown on both the income statement and the statement of owner's equity.

T   F   **7.** The collection of cash from accounts receivable increases owner's equity.

T   F   **8.** Expenses decrease owner's equity.

T   F   **9.** Revenue decreases owner's equity.

T   F   **10.** When equipment is purchased for cash, there is no change in the total value of the firm's property.

Part B Matching   *For each numbered item, choose the matching term from the box and write the identifying letter in the answer column.*

_____   **1.** Property owned by a business.

_____   **2.** A business obligation or debt.

_____   **3.** Owner's financial interest in the business.

_____   **4.** Those to whom money is owed.

_____   **5.** An expression of the relationship in which assets equal liabilities plus owner's equity.

_____   **6.** Inflows of money or other assets resulting from sales of goods or service.

_____   **7.** Amount remaining when total revenue is more than total expenses.

_____   **8.** Amounts owed by charge account customers.

> **a.** Accounts Receivable
> **b.** Assets
> **c.** Creditors
> **d.** Revenue
> **e.** Owner's equity
> **f.** Liability
> **g.** Net income
> **h.** Fundamental accounting equation

Part C Completion   *In the answer column, supply the missing word or words needed to complete each of the following statements.*

_____   **1.** The basic reason for starting a business is the possibility of making a _____.

_____   **2.** Accounts receivable result when goods are sold or services are performed on _____ ___ _____.

_____   **3.** When expenses are paid, the owner's equity is _____.

_____   **4.** Regardless of the number and variety of transactions, liabilities plus owner's equity always equal _____.

_____   **5.** When supplies are first purchased for use in operations, they are considered a type of _____.

_____   **6.** When property values and financial interest increase or decrease, the sum of the items on both sides of the equation always remains _____.

_____   **7.** The purchase of new equipment on account creates a debt that is called a(n) _____ _____ or _____.

_____   **8.** Accountants must _____ each business transaction before they can intelligently record, report, and interpret it.

Demonstration Problem

The account balances for Eugene Henderson, CPA, for the month of January 2016 are shown below in random order.

Rent Expense	$ 9,000	Advertising Expense	$ 7,250
Fees Earned	145,200	Office Equipment	58,640
Accounts Payable	30,440	T. Neal, Drawing	18,000
Salaries Expense	25,800	Accounts Receivable	32,475
Cash	190,674	E. Henderson, Capital 1/1	?

Instructions

1. Determine the balance for **Eugene Henderson, Capital,** on January 1, 2016.
2. Prepare an income statement, a statement of owner's equity, and a balance sheet as of January 31, 2016.
3. List the expenses on the income statement in alphabetical order.

SOLUTION

Determine the balance for Eugene Henderson Capital, on January 1, 2016.
Let Thomas Neal, Capital = X. Solving for X:

	Assets			=	Liabilities +		Owner's Equity			
	Accts.		Office		Accounts	E. Henderson				
Cash +	Rec. +		Equip.	=	Payable +	Capital −	Drawing +	Revenue −	Expenses	
190,674 +	32,475 +		58,640	=	30,440 +	X −	18,000 +	145,200 −	42,050	
			281,789	=	115,590 +	X				
	281,789 −		115,590	=	115,590 −	115,590 +	X			
			166,199	=	X					

Thomas Neal, Capital, January 1, 2013 = **$166,199**

Total Expenses:

Rent Expense	$ 9,000
Salaries Expense	25,800
Advertising Expense	7,250
	$42,050

Eugene Henderson, CPA
Income Statement
Month Ended January 31, 2016

Revenue			
Fees Earned			145 2 0 0 00
Expenses			
Rent Expense	9 0 0 0 00		
Salaries Expense	25 8 0 0 00		
Advertising Expense	7 2 5 0 00		
Total Expenses			42 0 5 0 00
Net Income			103 1 5 0 00

Eugene Henderson, CPA
Statement of Owner's Equity
Month Ended January 31, 2016

Eugene Henderson, Capital, January 1, 2016			166 1 9 9 00
Net Income	103 1 5 0 00		
Less Withdrawals	18 0 0 0 00		
Increase in Capital			85 1 5 0 00
Eugene Henderson, Capital, January 31, 2016			251 3 4 9 00

SOLUTION (continued)

Eugene Henderson, CPA

Balance Sheet

January 31, 2016

Assets						Liabilities					
Cash	190	6	7	4	00	Accounts Payable	30	4	4	0	00
Accounts Receivable	32	4	7	5	00	Owner's Equity					
Office Equipment	58	6	4	0	00	Eugene Henderson, Capital	251	3	4	9	00
Total Assets	281	7	8	9	00	Total Liabilities and Owner's Equity	281	7	8	9	00

WORKING PAPERS

Name _____

EXERCISE 2.1

Assets   _____

Liabilities   _____

Owner's Equity _____

EXERCISE 2.2

1. _____

2. _____

3. _____

4. _____

5. _____

EXERCISE 2.3

	Assets	=	Liabilities	+	Owner's Equity
1.	_____	=	_____	+	_____
2.	_____	=	_____	+	_____
3.	_____	=	_____	+	_____
4.	_____	=	_____	+	_____
5.	_____	=	_____	+	_____

EXERCISE 2.4

Transaction	Assets	=	Liabilities	+	Owner's Equity
1.	____ + ____	=	_____	+	____ + ____
2.	_____	=	_____	+	_____
3.	_____	=	_____	+	_____
4.	_____	=	_____	+	_____
5.	_____	=	_____	+	_____

Name _____

EXERCISE 2.5

	Assets		=	Liabilities	+	Owner's Equity		
Cash	+ Accounts Receivable	+ Equipment	=	Accounts Payable	+	Amos Roberts Capital	+ Revenue	− Expenses
1.								
2.								
3.								
4.								
5.								
6.								
7.								
8.								
Totals	+	+	=	+	+	−		

EXERCISE 2.6

_____

Revenue

_____

Expenses

_____

EXERCISE 2.7

1. _____
2. _____
3. _____
4. _____
5. _____
6. _____
7. _____

EXERCISE 2.8

_____

_____

_____

EXERCISE 2.9

_____

Revenue

_____

Expenses

_____

_____

_____

_____

_____

EXERCISE 2.10

PROBLEM 2.1A or 2.1B

	Cash	+	Accounts Receivable	+	Supplies	+	Equipment	=	Accounts Payable	+	Owner's Capital
					Assets			= Liabilities		+ Owner's Equity	
1.											
2.											
3.											
4.											
5.											
6.											
7.											
8.											
9.											
10.											
11.											
Totals		+		+		+		=		+	

Analyze: _____

_____

PROBLEM 2.2A or 2.2B

	Assets				= Liabilities +		Owner's Equity		
	Cash	+ Accounts Receivable +	+		= Accounts Payable +	Capital +	Revenue −	Expenses
Beginning Balances	_____ +	_____ +	_____ +	_____	= _____ +	_____ +	_____ −	_____
1.	_____	_____	_____	_____	_____	_____	_____	_____
New Balances	_____ +	_____ +	_____ +	_____	= _____ +	_____ +	_____ −	_____
2.	_____	_____	_____	_____	_____	_____	_____	_____
New Balances	_____ +	_____ +	_____ +	_____	= _____ +	_____ +	_____ −	_____
3.	_____	_____	_____	_____	_____	_____	_____	_____
New Balances	_____ +	_____ +	_____ +	_____	= _____ +	_____ +	_____ −	_____
4.	_____	_____	_____	_____	_____	_____	_____	_____
New Balances	_____ +	_____ +	_____ +	_____	= _____ +	_____ +	_____ −	_____
5.	_____	_____	_____	_____	_____	_____	_____	_____
New Balances	_____ +	_____ +	_____ +	_____	= _____ +	_____ +	_____ −	_____
6.	_____	_____	_____	_____	_____	_____	_____	_____
New Balances	_____ +	_____ +	_____ +	_____	= _____ +	_____ +	_____ −	_____
7.	_____	_____	_____	_____	_____	_____	_____	_____
New Balances	_____ +	_____ +	_____ +	_____	= _____ +	_____ +	_____ −	_____
8.	_____	_____	_____	_____	_____	_____	_____	_____
New Balances	_____ +	_____ +	_____ +	_____	= _____ +	_____ +	_____ −	_____
9.	_____	_____	_____	_____	_____	_____	_____	_____
New Balances	_____ +	_____ +	_____ +	_____	= _____ +	_____ +	_____ −	_____
10.	_____	_____	_____	_____	_____	_____	_____	_____
New Balances	_____ +	_____ +	_____ +	_____	= _____ +	_____ +	_____ −	_____

Analyze: _____

_____

Name _____

PROBLEM 2.3A or 2.3B

_____

_____

Analyze: _____

_____

PROBLEM 2.4A or 2.4B

_____

_____

PROBLEM 2.4A or 2.4B (continued)

Analyze: _____

CRITICAL THINKING PROBLEM 2.1

Determine the balance for **Carl Nicholson**, April 30, 2016.

Assets			= Liabilities +		Owner's Equity		
Cash	+ Accounts Receivable	+ Machinery	= Accounts Payable	+ D. Garcia Capital	− D. Garcia Drawing	+ Revenue	− Expenses
$30,000	+ $12,000	+ $21,000	= $13,200	+ ?	− $6,800	+ $26,800	− $21,490

Let Carl Nicholson, Capital = X.

Solving for X:

Carl Nicholson, Capital, April 1, 2016, = _____

Advertising Expense	$ 3,890
Maintenance Expense	4,600
Salaries Expense	13,000
Total Expenses	

CRITICAL THINKING PROBLEM 2.1 (continued)

Analyze: _____

_____

Chapter 2 Practice Test Answer Key

Part A True-False

1. T	6. T
2. T	7. F
3. F	8. T
4. T	9. F
5. F	10. T

Part B Matching

1. b	5. h
2. f	6. d
3. e	7. g
4. c	8. a

Part C Completion

1. profit
2. credit or on account
3. reduced or decreased
4. assets
5. asset or property
6. equal
7. accounts payable or liability
8. analyze

CRITICAL THINKING PROBLEM 2.2

CHAPTER 3

Analyzing Business Transactions Using T Accounts

STUDY GUIDE

Understanding the Chapter

Objectives

1. Set up T accounts for assets, liabilities, and owner's equity. **2.** Analyze business transactions and enter them in the accounts. **3.** Determine the balance of an account. **4.** Set up T accounts for revenue and expenses. **5.** Prepare a trial balance from T accounts. **6.** Prepare an income statement, a statement of owner's equity, and a balance sheet. **7.** Develop a chart of accounts. **8.** Define the accounting terms new to this chapter.

Reading Assignment

Read Chapter 3 in the textbook. Complete the textbook Section Self Review as you finish reading each section of the chapter, and the Comprehensive Self Review at the end of the chapter. Refer to the Chapter 3 Glossary or to the Glossary at the end of the book to find definitions for terms that are not familiar to you.

Activities

❏ **Thinking Critically**

Answer the *Thinking Critically* questions for AT&T and Managerial Implications.

❏ **Discussion Questions**

Answer each assigned discussion question in Chapter 3.

❏ **Exercises**

Complete each assigned exercise in Chapter 3. Use the forms provided in this SGWP. The objectives covered by an exercise are given after the exercise number. If you need help with an exercise, review the portion of the chapter related to the objective(s) covered.

❏ **Problems A/B**

Complete each assigned problem in Chapter 3. Use the forms provided in this SGWP. The objectives covered by a problem are given after the problem number. If you need help with a problem, review the portion of the chapter related to the objective(s) covered.

❏ **Critical Thinking Problems**

Complete the critical thinking problems as assigned. Use the forms provided in this SGWP.

❏ **Business Connections**

Complete the Business Connections activities as assigned to gain a deeper understanding of Chapter 3 concepts.

Practice Tests

Complete the Practice Tests, which cover the main points in your reading assignment. Compare your answers with those in the Practice Test Answer Key for Chapter 3 at the end of this chapter. If you have answered any questions incorrectly, review the related section of the text.

Part A True-False *For each of the following statements, circle T in the answer column if the answer is true or F if the answer is false.*

T	F	**1.**	An entry on the left side of any account is called a debit.
T	F	**2.**	Revenue accounts are increased by credits.
T	F	**3.**	Decreases in liabilities are credited to the liability account.
T	F	**4.**	Increases in liabilities are recorded on the debit side of an account.
T	F	**5.**	Decreases in assets are recorded on the left side of an account.
T	F	**6.**	Increases in assets are recorded on the debit side of an account.
T	F	**7.**	Increases in expense accounts are recorded by credit entries.
T	F	**8.**	The owner's beginning investment is entered as a debit in the owner's capital account.
T	F	**9.**	The **Accounts Payable** account is decreased by a debit entry.
T	F	**10.**	A cash payment by a business is recorded as a debit entry in the **Cash** account.
T	F	**11.**	The receipt of cash is recorded by a debit entry to the **Cash** account.
T	F	**12.**	A reduction in the equity of the owner is recorded by making a debit entry in the **Owner's Drawing** account.
T	F	**13.**	Accountants keep a separate record for each asset, liability, and owner's equity item.
T	F	**14.**	The T account allows increases and decreases to be separated and recorded on different sides.
T	F	**15.**	An increase in the owner's investment is recorded by crediting the owner's capital account.

Part B Matching

For each numbered item, choose the matching item from the box and write the identifying letter in the answer column.

_____ 1. An entry on the left side of an account.

_____ 2. An entry on the right side of an account.

_____ 3. A system for arranging accounts in logical order.

_____ 4. An operating cost that decreases owner's equity.

_____ 5. The system of accounting that requires equality of the entries on each side of the equation.

_____ 6. Accounts whose balances are carried forward to start a new period.

_____ 7. Accounts whose balances are transferred to a summary account at the end of the accounting period.

_____ 8. A subdivision of owner's equity that is used to record various types of income of a business.

_____ 9. A separate written record that is kept for each asset, liability, and owner's equity item.

a. Account
b. Double-entry system
c. Credit
d. Permanent accounts
e. Temporary accounts
f. Expense
g. Revenue
h. Chart of accounts
i. Debit

Part C Completion

In the answer column, supply the missing word or words needed to complete each of the following statements.

_____ 1. The _____ _____ is a statement prepared to test the accuracy of the figures recorded in the accounts.

_____ 2. The _____ _____ of an account is where increases in the account are recorded and where the balance is recorded.

_____ 3. A(n) _____ is the total of several entries on either side of an account that is entered in small pencil.

_____ 4. A(n) _____ is an error where the digits of a number are switched.

_____ 5. A(n) _____ is an error where the decimal point is misplaced.

Demonstration Problem

Anita Thomas is an investment broker who operates her own business, Thomas Investment Counseling.

Instructions

1. Analyze the transactions for the month of January 2016, and record each in the appropriate T accounts. Use plus and minus signs to show increases and decreases. Identify each entry in the T accounts by writing the number of the transaction next to the entry.

2. Determine the balance for each T account. Prepare a trial balance.

Transactions

1. Anita Thomas invested $100,000 in cash to start the business.

2. Thomas Investment Counseling purchased office furniture for $20,000 on account.

3. Paid $7,500 for one month's rent.

4. Sold an investment portfolio to the Darden Family and received fees of $75,000.

5. Purchased a computer for $2,500, paying $1,250 in cash and putting the balance on account for 60 days.

6. Paid $10,200 for employee salaries.

7. Purchased office equipment for $16,800 with credit terms of 60 days.

8. Sold an investment portfolio to the Williams Family and will receive commission fees of $30,900 in 30 days.

9. Issued a check for $6,800 for partial payment of the amount for office equipment.

10. Anita Thomas withdrew $7,500 in cash for personal use.

11. Issued a check for $1,560 to pay the utility bill.

SOLUTION

Cash			
(1)	+ 100,000	(3)	− 7,500
(4)	+ 75,000	(5)	− 1,250
		(6)	− 10,200
		(9)	− 6,800
	175,000	(10)	− 7,500
		(11)	− 1,560
Bal.	140,190		34,810

Accounts Receivable	
(8)	+ 30,900

Office Furniture	
(2)	+ 20,000

Office Equipment	
(5)	+ 2,500
(7)	+ 16,800
Bal.	19,300

Accounts Payable			
(9)	− 6,800	(2)	+ 20,000
		(5)	+ 1,250
		(7)	+ 16,800
		Bal.	31,250

Anita Thomas, Capital		
	(1)	+ 100,000

Anita Thomas, Drawing	
(10)	+ 7,500

Fees Income		
	(4)	+ 75,000
	(8)	+ 30,900
	Bal.	105,900

Rent Expense	
(3)	+ 7,500

Salaries Expense	
(6)	+ 10,200

Utilities Expense	
(11)	+ 1,560

SOLUTION (continued)

Thomas Investment Counseling

Trial Balance

January 31, 2016

ACCOUNT NAME	DEBIT	CREDIT
Cash	140 1 9 0 00	
Accounts Receivable	30 9 0 0 00	
Office Furniture	20 0 0 0 00	
Office Equipment	19 3 0 0 00	
Accounts Payable		31 2 5 0 00
Anita Thomas, Capital		100 0 0 0 00
Anita Thomas, Drawing	7 5 0 0 00	
Fees Income		105 9 0 0 00
Rent Expense	7 5 0 0 00	
Salaries Expense	10 2 0 0 00	
Utilities Expense	1 5 6 0 00	
Totals	237 1 5 0 00	237 1 5 0 00

WORKING PAPERS

Name _____

EXERCISE 3.1

EXERCISE 3.2

EXERCISE 3.3

1. _____   5. _____

2. _____   6. _____

3. _____   7. _____

4. _____   8. _____

Name _____

EXERCISE 3.4

1. _____
2. _____
3. _____
4. _____
5. _____

EXERCISE 3.5

_____   _____
_____   _____
_____   _____
_____   _____
_____   _____

EXERCISE 3.6

_____

ACCOUNT NAME	DEBIT	CREDIT

EXERCISE 3.6 (continued)

EXERCISE 3.7

EXERCISE 3.7 (continued)

EXERCISE 3.8

Name _____

PROBLEM 3.1A or 3.1B

1. _____ | _____   _____ | _____

2. _____ | _____   _____ | _____

3. _____ | _____   _____ | _____

4. _____ | _____   _____ | _____

5. _____ | _____   _____ | _____

6. _____ | _____   _____ | _____

7. _____ | _____   _____ | _____

8. _____ | _____   _____ | _____

Analyze: _____

_____

PROBLEM 3.2A or 3.2B

1. _____ | _____   _____ | _____

2. _____ | _____   _____ | _____

3. _____ | _____   _____ | _____

4. _____ | _____   _____ | _____

5. _____ | _____   _____ | _____

6. _____ | _____   _____ | _____

7. _____ | _____   _____ | _____

8. _____ | _____   _____ | _____

Analyze: _____

_____

PROBLEM 3.3A or 3.3B

1. _____|_____   _____|_____

2. _____|_____   _____|_____

3. _____|_____   _____|_____

4. _____|_____   _____|_____

5. _____|_____   _____|_____

6. _____|_____   _____|_____

7. _____|_____   _____|_____

8. _____|_____   _____|_____

9. _____|_____   _____|_____

10. _____|_____   _____|_____

11. _____|_____   _____|_____

12. _____|_____   _____|_____

PROBLEM 3.4A or 3.4B

Analyze: _____

_____

PROBLEM 3.5A or 3.5B

ACCOUNT NAME	DEBIT	CREDIT

PROBLEM 3.5A or 3.5B (continued)

Analyze: _____

CRITICAL THINKING PROBLEM 3.1

CRITICAL THINKING PROBLEM 3.1 (continued)

CRITICAL THINKING PROBLEM 3.1 (continued)

_____

_____

_____

_____

_____

_____

_____

_____

_____

_____

_____

_____

_____

_____

_____

_____

_____

_____

_____

_____

_____

_____

_____

_____

_____

_____

_____

_____

_____

_____

_____

_____

_____

CRITICAL THINKING PROBLEM 3.2

CRITICAL THINKING PROBLEM 3.2 (continued)

ACCOUNT NAME	DEBIT	CREDIT

	DEBIT	CREDIT

Name _____

CRITICAL THINKING PROBLEM 3.2 (continued)

Analyze: _____

Chapter 3 Practice Test Answer Key

Part A True-False			Part B Matching		Part C Completion
1. T	6. T	11. T	1. i	6. d	1. trial balance
2. T	7. F	12. T	2. c	7. e	2. normal balance
3. F	8. F	13. T	3. h	8. g	3. footing
4. F	9. T	14. T	4. f	9. a	4. transposition
5. F	10. F	15. T	5. b		5. slide

CHAPTER 4

The General Journal and the General Ledger

STUDY GUIDE

Understanding the Chapter

Objectives	**1.** Record transactions in the general journal. **2.** Prepare compound journal entries. **3.** Post journal entries to general ledger accounts. **4.** Correct errors made in the journal or ledger. **5.** Define the accounting terms new to this chapter.
Reading Assignment	Read Chapter 4 in the textbook. Complete the textbook Section Self Review as you finish reading each section of the chapter, and the Comprehensive Self Review at the end of the chapter. Refer to the Chapter 4 Glossary or to the Glossary at the end of the book to find definitions for terms that are not familiar to you.

Activities

❏ **Thinking Critically**	Answer the *Thinking Critically* questions for Boeing and Managerial Implications.
❏ **Discussion Questions**	Answer each assigned discussion question in Chapter 4.
❏ **Exercises**	Complete each assigned exercise in Chapter 4. Use the forms provided in this SGWP. The objectives covered by an exercise are given after the exercise number. If you need help with an exercise, review the portion of the chapter related to the objective(s) covered.
❏ **Problems A/B**	Complete each assigned problem in Chapter 4. Use the forms provided in this SGWP. The objectives covered by a problem are given after the problem number. If you need help with a problem, review the portion of the chapter related to the objective(s) covered.
❏ **Critical Thinking Problems**	Complete the critical thinking problems as assigned. Use the forms provided in this SGWP.
❏ **Business Connections**	Complete the Business Connections activities as assigned to gain a deeper understanding of Chapter 4 concepts.

Practice Tests

Complete the Practice Tests, which cover the main points in your reading assignment. Compare your answers with those in the Practice Test Answer Key for Chapter 4 at the end of this chapter. If you have answered any questions incorrectly, review the related section of the text.

Part A Matching *For each numbered item, choose the matching term from the box and write the identifying letter in the answer column.*

_____ 1. Record of original entry.

_____ 2. The process of recording transactions in the journal.

_____ 3. Invoices and other business forms that contain the original data about transactions.

_____ 4. A chain of references that makes it possible to trace information about transactions through an accounting system.

_____ 5. A ledger account form that always shows the current balance of an account.

_____ 6. A journal entry that consists of more than one debit or more than one credit.

_____ 7. A permanent, classified record of all accounts used by a business.

_____ 8. Used to analyze transactions but not used to maintain financial records.

_____ 9. The process of transferring information from the journal to the ledger.

_____ 10. An entry that is made when there is an error in data that has been journalized and posted.

a. journal
b. source documents
c. posting
d. general ledger
e. T accounts
f. journalizing
g. correcting entry
h. compound entry
i. balance ledger form
j. audit trail

Part B Completion *In the answer column, supply the missing word or words needed to complete each of the following statements.*

_____ 1. All the accounts together constitute a(n) _____, or a record of final entry.

_____ 2. Notations that allow the data in journals and ledgers to be easily traced are called _____ _____.

_____ 3. Descriptions in the general journal should be complete but _____ ___ _____.

_____ 4. On the balance ledger form the second money column is used to record _____ amounts.

_____ 5. On the balance ledger form the first money column is used to record _____ amounts.

_____ 6. The accountant always records the _____ items first in the Description column of the journal.

_____ 7. The _____ is always entered at the top of the Date column.

_____ 8. The accountant enters transactions in the general journal in _____ or _____ order.

_____ 9. The pages in the ledger are usually organized so that the _____ or _____ _____ _____ come first.

_____ 10. If an error is discovered in a journal before the entry is _____, the error can be neatly crossed out and the correct data written above it.

Demonstration Problem

On January 1, 2016, Herschel Anderson opened his consulting office and began business as Anderson Consulting Services. Selected transactions for the first month of operations follow.

Instructions

1. Journalize the transactions on page 1 of a general journal. Write the year at the top of the Date column; include an explanation for each entry.

2. Post to the general ledger accounts. Use account numbers from accounts in working papers in General Ledger.

3. Prepare a trial balance.

DATE	TRANSACTIONS
January 1	Herschel Anderson invested $120,000 cash in the business.
2	Issued Check 101 for $7,500 to pay the January rent.
5	Purchased office equipment for $38,000 from Oxford Office Supply, Invoice 7045; issued Check 102 for $18,000 down payment with the balance due in 30 days.
12	Wrote a lease contract for Neal Davis for $7,000 cash.
15	Performed consulting services for a client, Williams Supply Company, for $25,000 to be received in 30 days.
28	Issued Check 103 for $12,000 for payment to Oxford Office Supply.
29	Issued Check 104 for $15,000 to Herschel Anderson for personal use.
31	Received $15,000 from Williams Supply Company for partial payment of its account.

SOLUTION

GENERAL JOURNAL

PAGE _____1_____

	DATE		DESCRIPTION	POST. REF.	DEBIT	CREDIT	
1	2016						1
2	Jan.	1	Cash	101	120 0 0 0 00		2
3			Herschel Anderson Capital	301		120 0 0 0 00	3
4			Investment to start business				4
5							5
6		2	Rent Expense	514	7 5 0 0 00		6
7			Cash	101		7 5 0 0 00	7
8			Issued Check 101 for January rent				8
9							9
10		5	Office Equipment	131	38 0 0 0 00		10
11			Cash	101		18 0 0 0 00	11
12			Accounts Payable	202		20 0 0 0 00	12
13			Issued Check 102 for office equipment,				13
14			balance due in 30 days.				14
15							15
16		12	Cash	101	7 0 0 0 00		16
17			Fees Income	401		7 0 0 0 00	17
18			Performed services for cash.				18
19							19
20		15	Accounts Receivable	111	25 0 0 0 00		20
21			Fees Income	401		25 0 0 0 00	21
22			Performed services on account.				22
23							23
24		28	Accounts Payable	202	12 0 0 0 00		24
25			Cash	101		12 0 0 0 00	25
26			Paid Invoice 7045, Check 103				26
27							27
28		29	Herschel Anderson, Drawing	302	15 0 0 0 00		28
29			Cash	101		15 0 0 0 00	29
30			Issued Check 104 to owner for personal use.				30
31							31
32		31	Cash	101	15 0 0 0 00		32
33			Accounts Receivable	111		15 0 0 0 00	33
34			Received partial payment				34
35			from Williams Supply Company				35
36							36
37							37
38							38
39							39

SOLUTION (continued)

GENERAL LEDGER

ACCOUNT __Cash__   **ACCOUNT NO.** __101__

DATE		DESCRIPTION	POST. REF.	DEBIT	CREDIT	BALANCE DEBIT	BALANCE CREDIT
2016							
Jan.	1		J1	120 0 0 0 00		120 0 0 0 00	
	2		J1		7 5 0 0 00	112 5 0 0 00	
	5		J1		18 0 0 0 00	94 5 0 0 00	
	12		J1	7 0 0 0 00		101 5 0 0 00	
	28		J1		12 0 0 0 00	89 5 0 0 00	
	29		J1		15 0 0 0 00	74 5 0 0 00	
	31		J1	15 0 0 0 00		89 5 0 0 00	

ACCOUNT __Accounts Receivable__   **ACCOUNT NO.** __111__

DATE		DESCRIPTION	POST. REF.	DEBIT	CREDIT	BALANCE DEBIT	BALANCE CREDIT
2016							
Jan.	15		J1	25 0 0 0 00		25 0 0 0 00	
	31		J1		15 0 0 0 00	10 0 0 0 00	

ACCOUNT __Office Equipment__   **ACCOUNT NO.** __131__

DATE		DESCRIPTION	POST. REF.	DEBIT	CREDIT	BALANCE DEBIT	BALANCE CREDIT
2016							
Jan.	5		J1	38 0 0 0 00		38 0 0 0 00	

ACCOUNT __Accounts Payable__   **ACCOUNT NO.** __202__

DATE		DESCRIPTION	POST. REF.	DEBIT	CREDIT	BALANCE DEBIT	BALANCE CREDIT
2016							
Jan.	5		J1		20 0 0 0 00		20 0 0 0 00
	28		J1	12 0 0 0 00			8 0 0 0 00

ACCOUNT __Herschel Anderson, Capital__   **ACCOUNT NO.** __301__

DATE		DESCRIPTION	POST. REF.	DEBIT	CREDIT	BALANCE DEBIT	BALANCE CREDIT
2016							
Jan.	1		J1		120 0 0 0 00		120 0 0 0 00

SOLUTION (continued)

ACCOUNT __Herschel Anderson, Drawing__   ACCOUNT NO. ___302___

DATE		DESCRIPTION	POST. REF.	DEBIT	CREDIT	BALANCE DEBIT	BALANCE CREDIT
2016							
Jan.	29		J1	15 0 0 0 00		15 0 0 0 00	

ACCOUNT __Fees Income__   ACCOUNT NO. ___401___

DATE		DESCRIPTION	POST. REF.	DEBIT	CREDIT	BALANCE DEBIT	BALANCE CREDIT
2016							
Jan.	12		J1		7 0 0 0 00		7 0 0 0 00
	15		J1		25 0 0 0 00		32 0 0 0 00

ACCOUNT __Rent Expense__   ACCOUNT NO. ___514___

DATE		DESCRIPTION	POST. REF.	DEBIT	CREDIT	BALANCE DEBIT	BALANCE CREDIT
2016							
Jan.	2		J1	7 5 0 0 00		7 5 0 0 00	

Anderson Consulting Services
Trial Balance
January 31, 2016

ACCOUNT NAME	DEBIT	CREDIT
Cash	89 5 0 0 00	
Accounts Receivable	10 0 0 0 00	
Office Equipment	38 0 0 0 00	
Accounts Payable		8 0 0 0 00
Herschel Anderson, Capital		120 0 0 0 00
Herschel Anderson, Drawing	15 0 0 0 00	
Fees Income		32 0 0 0 00
Rent Expense	7 5 0 0 00	
Totals	160 0 0 0 00	160 0 0 0 00

WORKING PAPERS

Name _____

EXERCISE 4.1

	Debit	Credit		Debit	Credit		Debit	Credit
1.			5.			8.		
2.			6.			9.		
3.			7.			10.		
4.								

EXERCISE 4.2

GENERAL JOURNAL

PAGE _____

	DATE	DESCRIPTION	POST. REF.	DEBIT	CREDIT	
1						1
2						2
3						3
4						4
5						5
6						6
7						7
8						8
9						9
10						10
11						11
12						12
13						13
14						14
15						15
16						16
17						17
18						18
19						19
20						20
21						21
22						22
23						23
24						24
25						25
26						26
27						27
28						28
29						29

EXERCISE 4.2 (continued)

GENERAL JOURNAL   PAGE _____

	DATE		DESCRIPTION	POST. REF.	DEBIT	CREDIT	
1							1
2							2
3							3
4							4
5							5
6							6
7							7
8							8
9							9
10							10
11							11
12							12
13							13
14							14
15							15
16							16

EXERCISE 4.3

GENERAL LEDGER

ACCOUNT _____ ACCOUNT NO. _____

DATE		DESCRIPTION	POST. REF.	DEBIT	CREDIT	BALANCE	
						DEBIT	CREDIT

EXERCISE 4.3 (continued)

GENERAL LEDGER

ACCOUNT _____ ACCOUNT NO. _____

DATE	DESCRIPTION	POST. REF.	DEBIT	CREDIT	BALANCE	
					DEBIT	CREDIT

ACCOUNT _____ ACCOUNT NO. _____

DATE	DESCRIPTION	POST. REF.	DEBIT	CREDIT	BALANCE	
					DEBIT	CREDIT

ACCOUNT _____ ACCOUNT NO. _____

DATE	DESCRIPTION	POST. REF.	DEBIT	CREDIT	BALANCE	
					DEBIT	CREDIT

ACCOUNT _____ ACCOUNT NO. _____

DATE	DESCRIPTION	POST. REF.	DEBIT	CREDIT	BALANCE	
					DEBIT	CREDIT

ACCOUNT _____ ACCOUNT NO. _____

DATE	DESCRIPTION	POST. REF.	DEBIT	CREDIT	BALANCE	
					DEBIT	CREDIT

Name _____

EXERCISE 4.3 (continued)

GENERAL LEDGER

ACCOUNT _____ ACCOUNT NO. _____

	DATE	DESCRIPTION	POST. REF.	DEBIT	CREDIT	BALANCE	
						DEBIT	CREDIT

ACCOUNT _____ ACCOUNT NO. _____

	DATE	DESCRIPTION	POST. REF.	DEBIT	CREDIT	BALANCE	
						DEBIT	CREDIT

ACCOUNT _____ ACCOUNT NO. _____

	DATE	DESCRIPTION	POST. REF.	DEBIT	CREDIT	BALANCE	
						DEBIT	CREDIT

ACCOUNT _____ ACCOUNT NO. _____

	DATE	DESCRIPTION	POST. REF.	DEBIT	CREDIT	BALANCE	
						DEBIT	CREDIT

ACCOUNT _____ ACCOUNT NO. _____

	DATE	DESCRIPTION	POST. REF.	DEBIT	CREDIT	BALANCE	
						DEBIT	CREDIT

ACCOUNT _____ ACCOUNT NO. _____

	DATE	DESCRIPTION	POST. REF.	DEBIT	CREDIT	BALANCE	
						DEBIT	CREDIT

EXERCISE 4.4

GENERAL JOURNAL

PAGE _____

	DATE		DESCRIPTION	POST. REF.	DEBIT	CREDIT	
1							1
2							2
3							3
4							4
5							5
6							6
7							7
8							8
9							9
10							10
11							11
12							12
13							13
14							14
15							15
16							16
17							17
18							18
19							19
20							20
21							21
22							22
23							23
24							24
25							25
26							26
27							27
28							28
29							29
30							30
31							31
32							32
33							33
34							34
35							35
36							36
37							37

EXERCISE 4.5

GENERAL JOURNAL   PAGE _____

	DATE		DESCRIPTION	POST. REF.	DEBIT	CREDIT	
1							1
2							2
3							3
4							4
5							5
6							6

EXERCISE 4.6

GENERAL JOURNAL   PAGE _____

	DATE		DESCRIPTION	POST. REF.	DEBIT	CREDIT	
1							1
2							2
3							3
4							4
5							5
6							6

EXTRA FORM

GENERAL JOURNAL   PAGE _____

	DATE		DESCRIPTION	POST. REF.	DEBIT	CREDIT	
1							1
2							2
3							3
4							4
5							5
6							6
7							7
8							8
9							9
10							10
11							11
12							12
13							13

PROBLEM 4.1A or 4.1B

GENERAL JOURNAL

PAGE _____

	DATE		DESCRIPTION	POST. REF.	DEBIT	CREDIT	
1							1
2							2
3							3
4							4
5							5
6							6
7							7
8							8
9							9
10							10
11							11
12							12
13							13
14							14
15							15
16							16
17							17
18							18
19							19
20							20
21							21
22							22
23							23
24							24
25							25
26							26
27							27
28							28
29							29
30							30
31							31
32							32
33							33
34							34
35							35
36							36
37							37
38							38

PROBLEM 4.1A or 4.1B (continued)

GENERAL JOURNAL   PAGE _____

	DATE	DESCRIPTION	POST. REF.	DEBIT	CREDIT	
1						1
2						2
3						3
4						4
5						5
6						6
7						7
8						8
9						9
10						10
11						11
12						12
13						13
14						14
15						15
16						16
17						17
18						18
19						19
20						20
21						21
22						22
23						23
24						24
25						25
26						26
27						27
28						28
29						29
30						30
31						31
32						32
33						33
34						34
35						35
36						36
37						37

Analyze: _____

PROBLEM 4.2A or 4.2B

GENERAL JOURNAL

PAGE _____

	DATE		DESCRIPTION	POST. REF.	DEBIT	CREDIT	
1							1
2							2
3							3
4							4
5							5
6							6
7							7
8							8
9							9
10							10
11							11
12							12
13							13
14							14
15							15
16							16
17							17
18							18
19							19
20							20
21							21
22							22
23							23
24							24
25							25
26							26
27							27
28							28
29							29
30							30
31							31
32							32
33							33
34							34
35							35
36							36
37							37

PROBLEM 4.2A or 4.2B (continued)

GENERAL JOURNAL   PAGE _____

	DATE	DESCRIPTION	POST. REF.	DEBIT	CREDIT	
1						1
2						2
3						3
4						4
5						5
6						6
7						7
8						8
9						9
10						10
11						11
12						12
13						13
14						14
15						15
16						16
17						17
18						18
19						19
20						20
21						21
22						22
23						23
24						24
25						25
26						26
27						27
28						28
29						29
30						30
31						31
32						32
33						33
34						34
35						35
36						36
37						37

Name _____

PROBLEM 4.2A or 4.2B (continued)

GENERAL LEDGER

ACCOUNT _____ ACCOUNT NO. _____

DATE	DESCRIPTION	POST. REF.	DEBIT	CREDIT	BALANCE	
					DEBIT	CREDIT

ACCOUNT _____ ACCOUNT NO. _____

DATE	DESCRIPTION	POST. REF.	DEBIT	CREDIT	BALANCE	
					DEBIT	CREDIT

ACCOUNT _____ ACCOUNT NO. _____

DATE	DESCRIPTION	POST. REF.	DEBIT	CREDIT	BALANCE	
					DEBIT	CREDIT

ACCOUNT _____ ACCOUNT NO. _____

DATE	DESCRIPTION	POST. REF.	DEBIT	CREDIT	BALANCE	
					DEBIT	CREDIT

PROBLEM 4.2A or 4.2B (continued)

GENERAL LEDGER

ACCOUNT _____ ACCOUNT NO. _____

DATE	DESCRIPTION	POST. REF.	DEBIT	CREDIT	BALANCE	
					DEBIT	CREDIT

ACCOUNT _____ ACCOUNT NO. _____

DATE	DESCRIPTION	POST. REF.	DEBIT	CREDIT	BALANCE	
					DEBIT	CREDIT

ACCOUNT _____ ACCOUNT NO. _____

DATE	DESCRIPTION	POST. REF.	DEBIT	CREDIT	BALANCE	
					DEBIT	CREDIT

ACCOUNT _____ ACCOUNT NO. _____

DATE	DESCRIPTION	POST. REF.	DEBIT	CREDIT	BALANCE	
					DEBIT	CREDIT

ACCOUNT _____ ACCOUNT NO. _____

DATE	DESCRIPTION	POST. REF.	DEBIT	CREDIT	BALANCE	
					DEBIT	CREDIT

PROBLEM 4.2A or 4.2B (continued)

GENERAL LEDGER

ACCOUNT _____ ACCOUNT NO. _____

DATE	DESCRIPTION	POST. REF.	DEBIT	CREDIT	BALANCE	
					DEBIT	CREDIT

ACCOUNT _____ ACCOUNT NO. _____

DATE	DESCRIPTION	POST. REF.	DEBIT	CREDIT	BALANCE	
					DEBIT	CREDIT

ACCOUNT _____ ACCOUNT NO. _____

DATE	DESCRIPTION	POST. REF.	DEBIT	CREDIT	BALANCE	
					DEBIT	CREDIT

ACCOUNT _____ ACCOUNT NO. _____

DATE	DESCRIPTION	POST. REF.	DEBIT	CREDIT	BALANCE	
					DEBIT	CREDIT

ACCOUNT _____ ACCOUNT NO. _____

DATE	DESCRIPTION	POST. REF.	DEBIT	CREDIT	BALANCE	
					DEBIT	CREDIT

Analyze: _____

_____

PROBLEM 4.3A or 4.3B

_____

_____

_____

_____

_____

_____

Analyze: _____

_____

PROBLEM 4.4A or 4.4B

GENERAL JOURNAL   PAGE _____

	DATE	DESCRIPTION	POST. REF.	DEBIT	CREDIT	
1						1
2						2
3						3
4						4
5						5
6						6
7						7
8						8
9						9
10						10
11						11
12						12
13						13
14						14
15						15
16						16
17						17
18						18
19						19
20						20
21						21
22						22
23						23
24						24
25						25
26						26

PROBLEM 4.4A or 4.4B (continued)

GENERAL LEDGER

ACCOUNT _____ ACCOUNT NO. _____

DATE		DESCRIPTION	POST. REF.	DEBIT	CREDIT	BALANCE	
						DEBIT	CREDIT

ACCOUNT _____ ACCOUNT NO. _____

DATE		DESCRIPTION	POST. REF.	DEBIT	CREDIT	BALANCE	
						DEBIT	CREDIT

ACCOUNT _____ ACCOUNT NO. _____

DATE		DESCRIPTION	POST. REF.	DEBIT	CREDIT	BALANCE	
						DEBIT	CREDIT

ACCOUNT _____ ACCOUNT NO. _____

DATE		DESCRIPTION	POST. REF.	DEBIT	CREDIT	BALANCE	
						DEBIT	CREDIT

ACCOUNT _____ ACCOUNT NO. _____

DATE		DESCRIPTION	POST. REF.	DEBIT	CREDIT	BALANCE	
						DEBIT	CREDIT

PROBLEM 4.4A or 4.4B (continued)

GENERAL LEDGER

ACCOUNT _____ ACCOUNT NO. _____

	DATE	DESCRIPTION	POST. REF.	DEBIT	CREDIT	BALANCE	
						DEBIT	CREDIT

ACCOUNT _____ ACCOUNT NO. _____

	DATE	DESCRIPTION	POST. REF.	DEBIT	CREDIT	BALANCE	
						DEBIT	CREDIT

ACCOUNT _____ ACCOUNT NO. _____

	DATE	DESCRIPTION	POST. REF.	DEBIT	CREDIT	BALANCE	
						DEBIT	CREDIT

ACCOUNT _____ ACCOUNT NO. _____

	DATE	DESCRIPTION	POST. REF.	DEBIT	CREDIT	BALANCE	
						DEBIT	CREDIT

Analyze: _____

_____

EXTRA FORM

GENERAL LEDGER

ACCOUNT _____ ACCOUNT NO. _____

	DATE	DESCRIPTION	POST. REF.	DEBIT	CREDIT	BALANCE	
						DEBIT	CREDIT

CRITICAL THINKING PROBLEM 4.1

CRITICAL THINKING PROBLEM 4.1 (continued)

CRITICAL THINKING PROBLEM 4.2

GENERAL JOURNAL

	DATE	DESCRIPTION	POST. REF.	DEBIT	CREDIT	
1						1
2						2
3						3
4						4
5						5
6						6
7						7
8						8
9						9
10						10
11						11
12						12
13						13
14						14
15						15
16						16
17						17
18						18
19						19
20						20
21						21
22						22
23						23
24						24
25						25
26						26
27						27
28						28
29						29
30						30
31						31
32						32
33						33
34						34
35						35
36						36
37						37
38						38

CRITICAL THINKING PROBLEM 4.2 (continued)

GENERAL JOURNAL

PAGE _____

DATE	DESCRIPTION	POST. REF.	DEBIT	CREDIT	
1					1
2					2
3					3
4					4
5					5
6					6
7					7
8					8
9					9
10					10
11					11
12					12
13					13
14					14
15					15
16					16
17					17
18					18
19					19
20					20
21					21
22					22
23					23
24					24
25					25
26					26
27					27
28					28
29					29
30					30
31					31
32					32
33					33
34					34
35					35
36					36
37					37

CRITICAL THINKING PROBLEM 4.2 (continued)

GENERAL JOURNAL

PAGE _____

	DATE		DESCRIPTION	POST. REF.	DEBIT	CREDIT	
1							1
2							2
3							3
4							4
5							5
6							6
7							7
8							8
9							9
10							10
11							11
12							12
13							13
14							14

GENERAL LEDGER

ACCOUNT _____   ACCOUNT NO. _____

DATE	DESCRIPTION	POST. REF.	DEBIT	CREDIT	BALANCE	
					DEBIT	CREDIT

CRITICAL THINKING PROBLEM 4.2 (continued)

GENERAL LEDGER

ACCOUNT _____ ACCOUNT NO. _____

DATE	DESCRIPTION	POST. REF.	DEBIT	CREDIT	BALANCE	
					DEBIT	CREDIT

ACCOUNT _____ ACCOUNT NO. _____

DATE	DESCRIPTION	POST. REF.	DEBIT	CREDIT	BALANCE	
					DEBIT	CREDIT

ACCOUNT _____ ACCOUNT NO. _____

DATE	DESCRIPTION	POST. REF.	DEBIT	CREDIT	BALANCE	
					DEBIT	CREDIT

ACCOUNT _____ ACCOUNT NO. _____

DATE	DESCRIPTION	POST. REF.	DEBIT	CREDIT	BALANCE	
					DEBIT	CREDIT

ACCOUNT _____ ACCOUNT NO. _____

DATE	DESCRIPTION	POST. REF.	DEBIT	CREDIT	BALANCE	
					DEBIT	CREDIT

CRITICAL THINKING PROBLEM 4.2 (continued)

GENERAL LEDGER

ACCOUNT _____ ACCOUNT NO. _____

DATE	DESCRIPTION	POST. REF.	DEBIT	CREDIT	BALANCE	
					DEBIT	CREDIT

ACCOUNT _____ ACCOUNT NO. _____

DATE	DESCRIPTION	POST. REF.	DEBIT	CREDIT	BALANCE	
					DEBIT	CREDIT

ACCOUNT _____ ACCOUNT NO. _____

DATE	DESCRIPTION	POST. REF.	DEBIT	CREDIT	BALANCE	
					DEBIT	CREDIT

ACCOUNT _____ ACCOUNT NO. _____

DATE	DESCRIPTION	POST. REF.	DEBIT	CREDIT	BALANCE	
					DEBIT	CREDIT

ACCOUNT _____ ACCOUNT NO. _____

DATE	DESCRIPTION	POST. REF.	DEBIT	CREDIT	BALANCE	
					DEBIT	CREDIT

CRITICAL THINKING PROBLEM 4.2 (continued)

GENERAL LEDGER

ACCOUNT _____ ACCOUNT NO. _____

| DATE | DESCRIPTION | POST. REF. | DEBIT | CREDIT | BALANCE | |
					DEBIT	CREDIT

ACCOUNT _____ ACCOUNT NO. _____

| DATE | DESCRIPTION | POST. REF. | DEBIT | CREDIT | BALANCE | |
					DEBIT	CREDIT

ACCOUNT _____ ACCOUNT NO. _____

| DATE | DESCRIPTION | POST. REF. | DEBIT | CREDIT | BALANCE | |
					DEBIT	CREDIT

EXTRA FORMS

GENERAL LEDGER

ACCOUNT _____ ACCOUNT NO. _____

| DATE | DESCRIPTION | POST. REF. | DEBIT | CREDIT | BALANCE | |
					DEBIT	CREDIT

ACCOUNT _____ ACCOUNT NO. _____

| DATE | DESCRIPTION | POST. REF. | DEBIT | CREDIT | BALANCE | |
					DEBIT	CREDIT

CRITICAL THINKING PROBLEM 4.2 (continued)

ACCOUNT NAME	DEBIT	CREDIT

CRITICAL THINKING PROBLEM 4.2 (continued)

Analyze: _____

_____

Chapter 4 Practice Test Answer Key

Part A Matching

1. a	6. h		
2. f	7. d		
3. b	8. e		
4. j	9. c		
5. i	10. g		

Part B Completion

1. ledger
2. posting references
3. brief or concise
4. credit
5. debit
6. debit
7. year
8. chronological or date
9. assets or balance sheet accounts
10. posted

5

Adjustments and the Worksheet

STUDY GUIDE

Understanding the Chapter

Objectives	**1.** Complete a trial balance on a worksheet. **2.** Prepare adjustments for unrecorded business transactions. **3.** Complete the worksheet. **4.** Prepare an income statement, statement of owner's equity, and balance sheet from the completed worksheet. **5.** Journalize and post the adjusting entries. **6.** Define the accounting terms new to this chapter.
Reading Assignment	Read Chapter 5 in the textbook. Complete the textbook Section Self Review as you finish reading each section of the chapter, and the Comprehensive Self Review at the end of the chapter. Refer to the Chapter 5 Glossary or to the Glossary at the end of the book to find definitions for terms that are not familiar to you.

Activities

❑ **Thinking Critically**	Answer the *Thinking Critically* questions for Willamette Valley Vineyards and Managerial Implications.
❑ **Discussion Questions**	Answer each assigned discussion question in Chapter 5.
❑ **Exercises**	Complete each assigned exercise in Chapter 5. Use the forms provided in this SGWP. The objectives covered by an exercise are given after the exercise number. If you need help with an exercise, review the portion of the chapter related to the objective(s) covered.
❑ **Problems A/B**	Complete each assigned problem in Chapter 5. Use the forms provided in this SGWP. The objectives covered by a problem are given after the problem number. If you need help with a problem, review the portion of the chapter related to the objective(s) covered.
❑ **Critical Thinking Problems**	Complete the critical thinking problems as assigned. Use the forms provided in this SGWP.
❑ **Business Connections**	Complete the Business Connections activities as assigned to gain a deeper understanding of Chapter 5 concepts.

Practice Tests

Complete the Practice Tests, which cover the main points in your reading assignment. Compare your answers with those in the Practice Test Answer Key for Chapter 5 at the end of this chapter. If you have answered any questions incorrectly, review the related section of the text.

Part A True-False *For each of the following statements, circle T in the answer column if the statement is true or F if the statement is false.*

T   F   **1.** Liability account balances from the trial balance are normally transferred to the Balance Sheet credit column of the worksheet.

T   F   **2.** Asset account balances from the trial balance are normally transferred to the Income Statement Debit column of the worksheet.

T   F   **3.** The first two money columns of the worksheet contain a trial balance of the general ledger accounts.

T   F   **4.** Accountants use a worksheet as a means of organizing their figures quickly.

T   F   **5.** The ledger must be in balance before financial statements are prepared.

T   F   **6.** The Income Statement columns and Balance Sheet columns provide the figures for preparing the financial statements.

T   F   **7.** On a worksheet, the difference between the Debit and Credit Column totals in the Income Statement section must equal the difference between the Debit and Credit column totals in the Balance Sheet section.

T   F   **8.** After the net income (or net loss) is computed in the Income Statement section of the worksheet, this amount is transferred to the Balance Sheet section of the worksheet.

T   F   **9.** When the Balance Sheet columns of the worksheet are first added, the total of the Debit column should equal the total of the Credit column.

T   F   **10.** The balances of the expense accounts are normally transferred to the Income Statement Debit column of the worksheet.

Part B Matching *For each numbered item, choose the matching term from the box and write the identifying letter in the answer column.*

_____ 1. Assets = Liabilities + Owner's Equity.

_____ 2. A way to test the accuracy of the figures recorded in the general ledger.

_____ 3. The term used for an account with an excess of debits over credits.

_____ 4. The term used when the total of the debit amounts in the general ledger and the total of the credit amounts are equal.

_____ 5. The term used when referring to an account in which there is an excess of credits over debits.

_____ 6. A form used to organize the amounts needed to prepare the financial statements.

a. Worksheet
b. Trial balance
c. Debit balance
d. Fundamental accounting equation
e. Credit balance
f. In balance

Demonstration Problem

The general ledger accounts listed on the worksheet for the Atwell Graphics Design Company on January 31, 2016, show the results of the first month of operation.

Instructions

1. Record the following adjustments in the Adjustments section of the worksheet using the information below.

   a. Supplies used during the month, $4,425.

   b. The amount in the **Prepaid Rent** account represents a payment made on January 1 for the rent for 12 months.

   c. The equipment, purchased in January, has an estimated useful life of 10 years with no salvage value. The firm uses the straight-line method of depreciation.

2. Complete the worksheet.

3. Journalize and post the adjusting entries. Use journal page number 2. Use account numbers from accounts in working papers in General Ledger.

SOLUTION

Atwell Graphics Design Company
Worksheet
Month Ended January 31, 2016

Account Name	Trial Balance Debit	Trial Balance Credit	Adjustments Debit	Adjustments Credit	Adjusted Trial Balance Debit	Adjusted Trial Balance Credit	Income Statement Debit	Income Statement Credit	Balance Sheet Debit	Balance Sheet Credit
Cash	37,350.00				37,350.00				37,350.00	
Accounts Receivable	50,700.00				50,700.00				50,700.00	
Supplies	8,700.00			(a) 4,425.00	4,275.00				4,275.00	
Prepaid Rent	126,000.00			(b)10,500.00	115,500.00				115,500.00	
Equipment	126,000.00				126,000.00				126,000.00	
Accum. Depr.—Equipment				(c)1,050.00		1,050.00				1,050.00
Accounts Payable		80,400.00				80,400.00				80,400.00
John Atwell, Capital		147,600.00				147,600.00				147,600.00
John Atwell, Drawing	9,000.00				9,000.00				9,000.00	
Fees Income		226,515.00				226,515.00		226,515.00		
Advertising Expense	11,400.00				11,400.00		11,400.00			
Insurance Expense	12,000.00				12,000.00		12,000.00			
Salaries Expense	67,500.00				67,500.00		67,500.00			
Supplies Expense			(a) 4,425.00		4,425.00		4,425.00			
Rent Expense			(b)10,500.00		10,500.00		10,500.00			
Telephone Expense	2,625.00				2,625.00		2,625.00			
Utilities Expense	3,240.00				3,240.00		3,240.00			
Depr. Expense—Equipment			(c)1,050.00		1,050.00		1,050.00			
Totals	454,515.00	454,515.00	15,975.00	15,975.00	455,565.00	455,565.00	112,740.00	226,515.00	342,825.00	229,050.00
Net Income							113,775.00			113,775.00
							226,515.00	226,515.00	342,825.00	342,825.00

SOLUTION (continued)

GENERAL JOURNAL   PAGE ___2___

	DATE		DESCRIPTION	POST. REF.	DEBIT	CREDIT	
1			**Adjusting Entries**				1
2	2016						2
3	Jan.	31	Supplies Expense	518	4 4 2 5 00		3
4			Supplies	121		4 4 2 5 00	4
5							5
6		31	Rent Expense	519	1 0 5 0 0 00		6
7			Prepaid Rent	131		1 0 5 0 0 00	7
8							8
9		31	Depreciation Expense—Equipment	524	1 0 5 0 00		9
10			Accumulated Depreciation—Equipment	142		1 0 5 0 00	10
11							11

GENERAL LEDGER (PARTIAL)

ACCOUNT __Supplies__   ACCOUNT NO. ___121___

DATE		DESCRIPTION	POST. REF.	DEBIT	CREDIT	BALANCE DEBIT	BALANCE CREDIT
2016							
Jan.	3		J1	8 7 0 0 00		8 7 0 0 00	
	31	Adjusting	J2		4 4 2 5 00	4 2 7 5 00	

ACCOUNT __Prepaid Rent__   ACCOUNT NO. ___131___

DATE		DESCRIPTION	POST. REF.	DEBIT	CREDIT	BALANCE DEBIT	BALANCE CREDIT
2016							
Jan.	2		J1	126 0 0 0 00		126 0 0 0 00	
	31	Adjusting	J2		1 0 5 0 0 00	115 5 0 0 00	

ACCOUNT __Accumulated Depreciation—Equipment__   ACCOUNT NO. ___142___

DATE		DESCRIPTION	POST. REF.	DEBIT	CREDIT	BALANCE DEBIT	BALANCE CREDIT
2016							
Jan.	31	Adjusting	J2		1 0 5 0 00		1 0 5 0 00

SOLUTION (continued)

GENERAL LEDGER (PARTIAL)

ACCOUNT Supplies Expense   **ACCOUNT NO.** 518

DATE		DESCRIPTION	POST. REF.	DEBIT	CREDIT	BALANCE DEBIT	BALANCE CREDIT
2016							
Jan.	31	Adjusting	J2	4 4 2 5 00		4 4 2 5 00	

ACCOUNT Rent Expense   **ACCOUNT NO.** 519

DATE		DESCRIPTION	POST. REF.	DEBIT	CREDIT	BALANCE DEBIT	BALANCE CREDIT
2016							
Jan.	31	Adjusting	J2	10 5 0 0 00		10 5 0 0 00	

ACCOUNT Depreciation Expense—Equipment   **ACCOUNT NO.** 524

DATE		DESCRIPTION	POST. REF.	DEBIT	CREDIT	BALANCE DEBIT	BALANCE CREDIT
2016							
Jan.	31	Adjusting	J2	1 0 5 0 00		1 0 5 0 00	

WORKING PAPERS

Name _____

EXERCISE 5.1

1. _____
_____
_____
_____

2. _____
_____
_____
_____

3. _____
_____
_____
_____

EXERCISE 5.2

1. _____
_____
_____
_____

2. _____
_____
_____
_____

EXERCISE 5.3

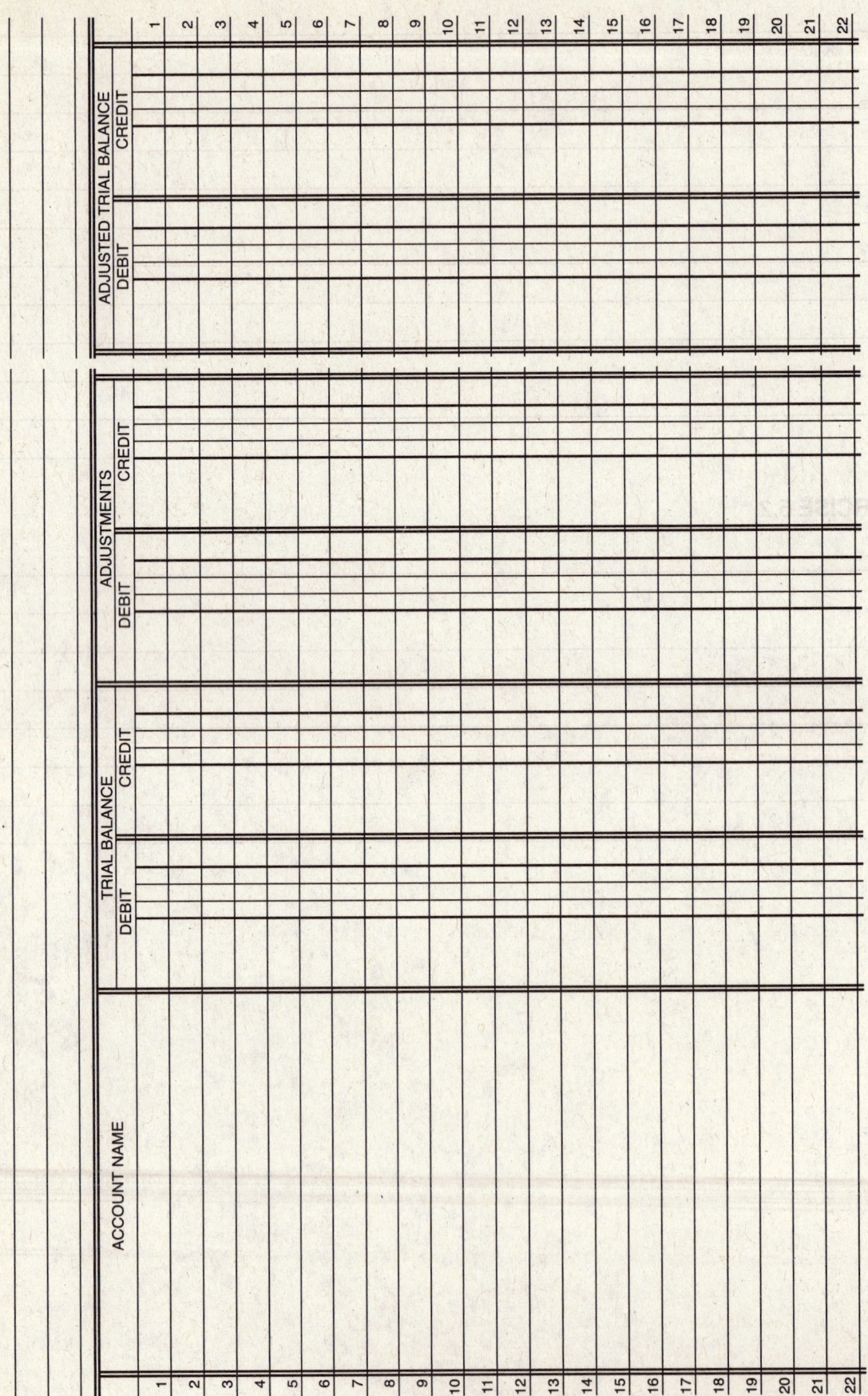

ACCOUNT NAME	TRIAL BALANCE		ADJUSTMENTS		ADJUSTED TRIAL BALANCE	
	DEBIT	CREDIT	DEBIT	CREDIT	DEBIT	CREDIT
1						
2						
3						
4						
5						
6						
7						
8						
9						
10						
11						
12						
13						
14						
15						
16						
17						
18						
19						
20						
21						
22						

EXERCISE 5.4

_____
_____
_____
_____
_____
_____
_____
_____
_____
_____
_____
_____
_____
_____
_____
_____

EXERCISE 5.5

GENERAL JOURNAL

PAGE _____

	DATE		DESCRIPTION	POST. REF.	DEBIT	CREDIT	
1							1
2							2
3							3
4							4
5							5
6							6
7							7
8							8
9							9
10							10
11							11

GENERAL LEDGER

ACCOUNT __Supplies__   ACCOUNT NO. ____121____

DATE	DESCRIPTION	POST. REF.	DEBIT	CREDIT	BALANCE	
					DEBIT	CREDIT

ACCOUNT __Prepaid Insurance__   ACCOUNT NO. ____131____

DATE	DESCRIPTION	POST. REF.	DEBIT	CREDIT	BALANCE	
					DEBIT	CREDIT

ACCOUNT __Accumulated Depreciation—Equipment__   ACCOUNT NO. ____142____

DATE	DESCRIPTION	POST. REF.	DEBIT	CREDIT	BALANCE	
					DEBIT	CREDIT

EXERCISE 5.5 (continued)

GENERAL LEDGER

ACCOUNT __Depreciation Expense—Equipment_____ ACCOUNT NO. ____517___

DATE	DESCRIPTION	POST. REF.	DEBIT	CREDIT	BALANCE	
					DEBIT	CREDIT

ACCOUNT __Insurance Expense_____ ACCOUNT NO. ____521___

DATE	DESCRIPTION	POST. REF.	DEBIT	CREDIT	BALANCE	
					DEBIT	CREDIT

ACCOUNT __Supplies Expense_____ ACCOUNT NO. ____523___

DATE	DESCRIPTION	POST. REF.	DEBIT	CREDIT	BALANCE	
					DEBIT	CREDIT

EXTRA FORMS

ACCOUNT _____ ACCOUNT NO. _____

DATE	DESCRIPTION	POST. REF.	DEBIT	CREDIT	BALANCE	
					DEBIT	CREDIT

ACCOUNT _____ ACCOUNT NO. _____

DATE	DESCRIPTION	POST. REF.	DEBIT	CREDIT	BALANCE	
					DEBIT	CREDIT

PROBLEM 5.1A or 5.1B

	ACCOUNT NAME	TRIAL BALANCE		ADJUSTMENTS	
		DEBIT	CREDIT	DEBIT	CREDIT
1					
2					
3					
4					
5					
6					
7					
8					
9					
10					
11					
12					
13					
14					
15					
16					
17					
18					
19					
20					
21					
22					
23					
24					
25					
26					
27					
28					
29					
30					
31					
32					

PROBLEM 5.1A or 5.1B (continued)

	ADJUSTED TRIAL BALANCE		INCOME STATEMENT		BALANCE SHEET		
	DEBIT	CREDIT	DEBIT	CREDIT	DEBIT	CREDIT	
							1
							2
							3
							4
							5
							6
							7
							8
							9
							10
							11
							12
							13
							14
							15
							16
							17
							18
							19
							20
							21
							22
							23
							24
							25
							26
							27
							28
							29
							30
							31
							32

Analyze: _____

PROBLEM 5.2A or 5.2B

	ACCOUNT NAME	TRIAL BALANCE		ADJUSTMENTS	
		DEBIT	CREDIT	DEBIT	CREDIT
1					
2					
3					
4					
5					
6					
7					
8					
9					
10					
11					
12					
13					
14					
15					
16					
17					
18					
19					
20					
21					
22					
23					
24					
25					
26					
27					
28					
29					
30					
31					
32					

Name _____

PROBLEM 5.2A or 5.2B (continued)

_____

	ADJUSTED TRIAL BALANCE		INCOME STATEMENT		BALANCE SHEET		
	DEBIT	CREDIT	DEBIT	CREDIT	DEBIT	CREDIT	
							1
							2
							3
							4
							5
							6
							7
							8
							9
							10
							12
							13
							14
							15
							16
							17
							18
							19
							20
							21
							22
							23
							24
							25
							26
							27
							28
							29
							30
							31
							32

Analyze: _____

PROBLEM 5.3A or 5.3B

PROBLEM 5.3A or 5.3B (continued)

_____
_____

Analyze: _____

_____

Name _____

PROBLEM 5.4A or 5.4B

	ACCOUNT NAME	TRIAL BALANCE		ADJUSTMENTS	
		DEBIT	CREDIT	DEBIT	CREDIT
1					
2					
3					
4					
5					
6					
7					
8					
9					
10					
11					
12					
13					
14					
15					
16					
17					
18					
19					
20					
21					
22					
23					
24					
25					
26					
27					
28					
29					
30					
31					
32					

PROBLEM 5.4A or 5.4B (continued)

ADJUSTED TRIAL BALANCE		INCOME STATEMENT		BALANCE SHEET		
DEBIT	CREDIT	DEBIT	CREDIT	DEBIT	CREDIT	
						1
						2
						3
						4
						5
						6
						7
						8
						9
						10
						11
						12
						13
						14
						15
						16
						17
						18
						19
						20
						21
						22
						23
						24
						25
						26
						27
						28
						29
						30
						31
						32

PROBLEM 5.4A or 5.4B (continued)

PROBLEM 5.4A or 5.4B (continued)

PROBLEM 5.4A or 5.4B (continued)

GENERAL JOURNAL   PAGE _____

	DATE		DESCRIPTION	POST. REF.	DEBIT	CREDIT	
1							1
2							2
3							3
4							4
5							5
6							6
7							7
8							8
9							9
10							10
11							11
12							12
13							13
14							14

GENERAL LEDGER

ACCOUNT _____   ACCOUNT NO. _____

DATE	DESCRIPTION	POST. REF.	DEBIT	CREDIT	BALANCE	
					DEBIT	CREDIT

ACCOUNT _____   ACCOUNT NO. _____

DATE	DESCRIPTION	POST. REF.	DEBIT	CREDIT	BALANCE	
					DEBIT	CREDIT

ACCOUNT _____   ACCOUNT NO. _____

DATE	DESCRIPTION	POST. REF.	DEBIT	CREDIT	BALANCE	
					DEBIT	CREDIT

PROBLEM 5.4A or 5.4B (continued)

GENERAL LEDGER

ACCOUNT _____ ACCOUNT NO. _____

DATE	DESCRIPTION	POST. REF.	DEBIT	CREDIT	BALANCE	
					DEBIT	CREDIT

ACCOUNT _____ ACCOUNT NO. _____

DATE	DESCRIPTION	POST. REF.	DEBIT	CREDIT	BALANCE	
					DEBIT	CREDIT

ACCOUNT _____ ACCOUNT NO. _____

DATE	DESCRIPTION	POST. REF.	DEBIT	CREDIT	BALANCE	
					DEBIT	CREDIT

ACCOUNT _____ ACCOUNT NO. _____

DATE	DESCRIPTION	POST. REF.	DEBIT	CREDIT	BALANCE	
					DEBIT	CREDIT

ACCOUNT _____ ACCOUNT NO. _____

DATE	DESCRIPTION	POST. REF.	DEBIT	CREDIT	BALANCE	
					DEBIT	CREDIT

Analyze: _____

_____

CRITICAL THINKING PROBLEM 5.1

_____

_____

	ACCOUNT NAME	TRIAL BALANCE		ADJUSTMENTS	
		DEBIT	CREDIT	DEBIT	CREDIT
1					
2					
3					
4					
5					
6					
7					
8					
9					
10					
11					
12					
13					
14					
15					
16					
17					
18					
19					
20					
21					
22					
23					
24					
25					
26					
27					
28					
29					
30					
31					
32					

CRITICAL THINKING PROBLEM 5.1 (continued)

_____
_____

	ADJUSTED TRIAL BALANCE		INCOME STATEMENT		BALANCE SHEET		
	DEBIT	CREDIT	DEBIT	CREDIT	DEBIT	CREDIT	
							1
							2
							3
							4
							5
							6
							7
							8
							9
							10
							11
							12
							13
							14
							15
							16
							17
							18
							19
							20
							21
							22
							23
							24
							25
							26
							27
							28
							29
							30
							31
							32

CRITICAL THINKING PROBLEM 5.1 (continued)

Name _____

CRITICAL THINKING PROBLEM 5.1 (continued)

CRITICAL THINKING PROBLEM 5.1 (continued)

GENERAL JOURNAL

PAGE _____

	DATE	DESCRIPTION	POST. REF.	DEBIT	CREDIT	
1						1
2						2
3						3
4						4
5						5
6						6
7						7
8						8
9						9
10						10
11						11

GENERAL LEDGER

ACCOUNT _____   ACCOUNT NO. _____

DATE	DESCRIPTION	POST. REF.	DEBIT	CREDIT	BALANCE	
					DEBIT	CREDIT

ACCOUNT _____   ACCOUNT NO. _____

DATE	DESCRIPTION	POST. REF.	DEBIT	CREDIT	BALANCE	
					DEBIT	CREDIT

ACCOUNT _____   ACCOUNT NO. _____

DATE	DESCRIPTION	POST. REF.	DEBIT	CREDIT	BALANCE	
					DEBIT	CREDIT

Name _____

CRITICAL THINKING PROBLEM 5.1 (continued)

GENERAL LEDGER

ACCOUNT _____ ACCOUNT NO. _____

DATE	DESCRIPTION	POST. REF.	DEBIT	CREDIT	BALANCE DEBIT	BALANCE CREDIT

ACCOUNT _____ ACCOUNT NO. _____

DATE	DESCRIPTION	POST. REF.	DEBIT	CREDIT	BALANCE DEBIT	BALANCE CREDIT

ACCOUNT _____ ACCOUNT NO. _____

DATE	DESCRIPTION	POST. REF.	DEBIT	CREDIT	BALANCE DEBIT	BALANCE CREDIT

Analyze: _____

EXTRA FORMS

ACCOUNT _____ ACCOUNT NO. _____

DATE	DESCRIPTION	POST. REF.	DEBIT	CREDIT	BALANCE DEBIT	BALANCE CREDIT

ACCOUNT _____ ACCOUNT NO. _____

DATE	DESCRIPTION	POST. REF.	DEBIT	CREDIT	BALANCE DEBIT	BALANCE CREDIT

CRITICAL THINKING PROBLEM 5.2

TO: _____

FROM: _____

DATE: _____

SUBJECT: _____

_____
_____
_____
_____
_____
_____
_____
_____
_____
_____
_____
_____
_____
_____
_____
_____
_____
_____
_____
_____
_____
_____
_____
_____

Chapter 5 Practice Test Answer Key

Part A True-False		Part B Matching	
1. T	6. T	1. d	4. f
2. F	7. T	2. b	5. e
3. T	8. T	3. c	6. a
4. T	9. F		
5. T	10. T		

Closing Entries and the Postclosing Trial Balance

STUDY GUIDE

Understanding the Chapter

Objectives	**1.** Journalize and post closing entries. **2.** Prepare a postclosing trial balance. **3.** Interpret financial statements. **4.** Review the steps in the accounting cycle. **5.** Define the accouning terms new to this chapter.
Reading Assignment	Read Chapter 6 in the textbook. Complete the textbook Section Self Review as you finish reading each section of the chapter, and the Comprehensive Self Review at the end of the chapter. Refer to the Chapter 6 Glossary or to the Glossary at the end of the book to find definitions for terms that are not familiar to you.

Activities

❏ **Thinking Critically**	Answer the *Thinking Critically* questions for Carnival Corporation and Managerial Implications.
❏ **Discussion Questions**	Answer each assigned discussion question in Chapter 6.
❏ **Exercises**	Complete each assigned exercise in Chapter 6. Use the forms provided in this SGWP. The objectives covered by an exercise are given after the exercise number. If you need help with an exercise, review the portion of the chapter related to the objective(s) covered.
❏ **Problems A/B**	Complete each assigned problem in Chapter 6. Use the forms provided in this SGWP. The objectives covered by a problem are given after the problem number. If you need help with a problem, review the portion of the chapter related to the objective(s) covered.
❏ **Critical Thinking Problems**	Complete the critical thinking problems as assigned. Use the forms provided in this SGWP.
❏ **Business Connections**	Complete the Business Connections activities as assigned to gain a deeper understanding of Chapter 6 concepts.

Practice Tests

Complete the Practice Tests, which cover the main points in your reading assignment. Compare your answers with those in the Practice Test Answer Key for Chapter 6 at the end of this chapter. If you have answered any questions incorrectly, review the related section of the text.

Part A True-False   *For each of the following statements, circle T in the answer column if the statement is true or F if the statement is false.*

T   F   **1.** All asset accounts are closed into the **Income Summary** account.

T   F   **2.** The balance of the **Income Summary** account—net income or net loss—is transferred to the owner's capital account.

T   F   **3.** The Income Summary is a financial statement prepared at the end of each accounting period.

T   F   **4.** Adjusting entries create a permanent record of any changes in account balances that are shown on the worksheet.

T   F   **5.** If an adjustment is not made for supplies used, the net income for the period will be understated.

T   F   **6.** Closing entries reduce the balance of revenue and asset accounts to zero so that they are ready to receive data for the next period.

T   F   **7.** The general ledger is a continuing record.

T   F   **8.** The postclosing trial balance will show figures for asset, liability, owner's equity, revenue, and expense accounts.

T   F   **9.** The total of all expenses appears on the credit side of the **Income Summary** account.

T   F   **10.** To close a revenue account, the accountant debits that account and credits the **Income Summary** account.

Part B Matching   *For each numbered item, choose the matching term from the box and write the identifying letter in the answer column.*

_____   **1.** The last step in the end-of-period procedure, which shows the accountant that it is safe to proceed with entries for the new period.

_____   **2.** Term used when referring to an account after its balance has been transferred out.

_____   **3.** Special account in the general ledger used for combining data about revenue and expenses.

_____   **4.** Journal entries used to transfer the balances of the revenue and expense accounts to the income summary account as part of the end-of-period procedures.

_____   **5.** The procedure of journalizing and posting the results of operations at the end of an accounting period.

a. Closing the accounting records
b. Closing entries
c. Closed account
d. Postclosing trial balance
e. Income Summary

104 ■ **Chapter 6**

Demonstration Problem

The Income Statement and Balance Sheet sections of the worksheet for Alexander Thomas for the period ended December 31, 2016 are shown below.

Instructions

1. Journalize the closing entries on page 24 of a general journal.

2. Determine the new balance for Capital once the closing entries have been posted.

Alexander Thomas

Worksheet

Month Ended December 31, 2016

	ACCOUNT NAME	INCOME STATEMENT DEBIT	INCOME STATEMENT CREDIT	BALANCE SHEET DEBIT	BALANCE SHEET CREDIT
1	Cash			48 0 0 0 00	
2	Accounts Receivable			3 0 0 0 00	
3	Supplies			6 0 0 0 00	
4	Prepaid Rent			4 5 0 0 00	
5	Equipment			30 0 0 0 00	
6	Accumulated Depreciation—Equipment				7 2 0 00
7	Accounts Payable				7 5 0 0 00
8	Alexander Thomas, Capital				54 7 5 0 00
9	Alexander Thomas, Drawing			3 0 0 0 00	
10	Fees Income		45 0 0 0 00		
11	Salaries Expense	7 2 0 0 00			
12	Utilities Expense	1 0 5 0 00			
13	Supplies Expense	2 4 0 0 00			
14	Advertising Expense	2 1 0 0 00			
15	Depreciation Expense—Equipment	7 2 0 00			
16	Totals	13 4 7 0 00	45 0 0 0 00	94 5 0 0 00	62 9 7 0 00
17	Net Income	31 5 3 0 00			31 5 3 0 00
18		45 0 0 0 00	45 0 0 0 00	94 5 0 0 00	94 5 0 0 00
19					

SOLUTION

GENERAL JOURNAL

PAGE ___24___

	DATE		DESCRIPTION	POST. REF.	DEBIT	CREDIT	
1			**Closing Entries**				1
2	2016						2
3	Dec.	31	**Fees Income**		45 0 0 0 00		3
4			**Income Summary**			45 0 0 0 00	4
5							5
6		31	**Income Summary**		13 4 7 0 00		6
7			**Salaries Expense**			7 2 0 0 00	7
8			**Utilities Expense**			1 0 5 0 00	8
9			**Supplies Expense**			2 4 0 0 00	9
10			**Advertising Expense**			2 1 0 0 00	10
11			**Depreciation Expense—Equipment**			7 2 0 00	11
12							12
13		31	**Income Summary**		31 5 3 0 00		13
14			**Alexander Thomas, Capital**			31 5 3 0 00	14
15							15
16		31	**Alexander Thomas, Capital**		3 0 0 0 00		16
17			**Alexander Thomas, Drawing**			3 0 0 0 00	17
18							18

New Capital Balance:

Alexander Thomas, Capital, December 1, 2016		$54,750.00
Add: Net Income	31,530.00	
Less Withdrawals for December	3,000.00	
Increase in Capital		28,530.00
Alexander Thomas, Capital, December 31, 2016		$83,280.00

WORKING PAPERS

Name _____

EXERCISE 6.1

GENERAL JOURNAL

PAGE _____

	DATE	DESCRIPTION	POST. REF.	DEBIT	CREDIT	
1						1
2						2
3						3
4						4
5						5
6						6
7						7
8						8
9						9
10						10
11						11
12						12
13						13
14						14
15						15
16						16
17						17
18						18
19						19
20						20
21						21

EXERCISE 6.2

1. _____
2. _____
3. _____
4. _____
5. _____
6. _____
7. _____
8. _____
9. _____

EXERCISE 6.3

1. _____   5. _____

2. _____   6. _____

3. _____   7. _____

4. _____

EXERCISE 6.4

1. _____   6. _____   11. _____

2. _____   7. _____   12. _____

3. _____   8. _____   13. _____

4. _____   9. _____   14. _____

5. _____   10. _____   15. _____

EXERCISE 6.5

1. Total revenue for the period is _____ .

2. Total expenses for the period are _____ .

3. Net income for the period is _____ .

4. Owner's withdrawals for the period are _____ .

EXERCISE 6.6

GENERAL JOURNAL

PAGE _____

	DATE		DESCRIPTION	POST. REF.	DEBIT	CREDIT	
1							1
2							2
3							3
4							4
5							5
6							6
7							7
8							8
9							9
10							10
11							11
12							12
13							13
14							14
15							15
16							16
17							17
18							18
19							19
20							20
21							21
22							22
23							23
24							24
25							25
26							26
27							27
28							28
29							29
30							30
31							31
32							32
33							33
34							34
35							35
36							36
37							37

Name _____

EXERCISE 6.6 (continued)

GENERAL LEDGER

ACCOUNT **Lee Retha Hale, Capital**   ACCOUNT NO. **301**

DATE		DESCRIPTION	POST. REF.	DEBIT	CREDIT	BALANCE DEBIT	BALANCE CREDIT
2016 Mar.	31	Balance	✔				80 0 0 0 00

ACCOUNT **Lee Retha Hale, Drawing**   ACCOUNT NO. **302**

DATE		DESCRIPTION	POST. REF.	DEBIT	CREDIT	BALANCE DEBIT	BALANCE CREDIT
2016 Mar.	31	Balance	✔			13 0 0 0 00	

ACCOUNT **Income Summary**   ACCOUNT NO. **399**

DATE	DESCRIPTION	POST. REF.	DEBIT	CREDIT	BALANCE DEBIT	BALANCE CREDIT

ACCOUNT **Fees Income**   ACCOUNT NO. **401**

DATE		DESCRIPTION	POST. REF.	DEBIT	CREDIT	BALANCE DEBIT	BALANCE CREDIT
2016 Mar.	31	Balance	✔				374 4 6 0 00

ACCOUNT **Depreciation Expense—Equipment**   ACCOUNT NO. **510**

DATE		DESCRIPTION	POST. REF.	DEBIT	CREDIT	BALANCE DEBIT	BALANCE CREDIT
2016 Mar.	31	Balance	✔			21 1 6 0 00	

110 ■ Chapter 6   Copyright © 2015 McGraw-Hill Education. All rights reserved.

EXERCISE 6.6 (continued)

GENERAL LEDGER

ACCOUNT __Insurance Expense__   ACCOUNT NO. ___511___

DATE		DESCRIPTION	POST. REF.	DEBIT	CREDIT	BALANCE DEBIT	BALANCE CREDIT
2016							
Mar.	31	Balance	✔			11 4 0 0 00	

ACCOUNT __Rent Expense__   ACCOUNT NO. ___514___

DATE		DESCRIPTION	POST. REF.	DEBIT	CREDIT	BALANCE DEBIT	BALANCE CREDIT
2016							
Mar.	31	Balance	✔			33 0 0 0 00	

ACCOUNT __Salaries Expense__   ACCOUNT NO. ___517___

DATE		DESCRIPTION	POST. REF.	DEBIT	CREDIT	BALANCE DEBIT	BALANCE CREDIT
2016							
Mar.	31	Balance	✔			166 0 0 0 00	

ACCOUNT __Supplies Expense__   ACCOUNT NO. ___518___

DATE		DESCRIPTION	POST. REF.	DEBIT	CREDIT	BALANCE DEBIT	BALANCE CREDIT
2016							
Mar.	31	Balance	✔			5 6 0 0 00	

ACCOUNT __Telephone Expense__   ACCOUNT NO. ___519___

DATE		DESCRIPTION	POST. REF.	DEBIT	CREDIT	BALANCE DEBIT	BALANCE CREDIT
2016							
Mar.	31	Balance	✔			6 8 0 0 00	

EXERCISE 6.6 (continued)

GENERAL LEDGER

ACCOUNT __Utilities Expense__ ACCOUNT NO. ___523___

DATE		DESCRIPTION	POST. REF.	DEBIT	CREDIT	BALANCE	
						DEBIT	CREDIT
2016							
Mar.	31	Balance	✔			9 4 0 0 00	

EXTRA FORMS

ACCOUNT _____ ACCOUNT NO. _____

DATE	DESCRIPTION	POST. REF.	DEBIT	CREDIT	BALANCE	
					DEBIT	CREDIT

ACCOUNT _____ ACCOUNT NO. _____

DATE	DESCRIPTION	POST. REF.	DEBIT	CREDIT	BALANCE	
					DEBIT	CREDIT

ACCOUNT _____ ACCOUNT NO. _____

DATE	DESCRIPTION	POST. REF.	DEBIT	CREDIT	BALANCE	
					DEBIT	CREDIT

EXERCISE 6.7

GENERAL JOURNAL   PAGE _____

	DATE		DESCRIPTION	POST. REF.	DEBIT	CREDIT	
1							1
2							2
3							3
4							4
5							5
6							6
7							7
8							8

EXERCISE 6.8

PROBLEM 6.1A or 6.1B

GENERAL JOURNAL   PAGE _____

	DATE	DESCRIPTION	POST. REF.	DEBIT	CREDIT	
1						1
2						2
3						3
4						4
5						5
6						6
7						7
8						8
9						9
10						10
11						11

GENERAL JOURNAL   PAGE _____

	DATE	DESCRIPTION	POST. REF.	DEBIT	CREDIT	
1						1
2						2
3						3
4						4
5						5
6						6
7						7
8						8
9						9
10						10
11						11
12						12
13						13
14						14
15						15
16						16
17						17
18						18
19						19
20						20

Analyze: _____

PROBLEM 6.2A or 6.2B

GENERAL JOURNAL

PAGE _____

	DATE		DESCRIPTION	POST. REF.	DEBIT	CREDIT	
1							1
2							2
3							3
4							4
5							5
6							6
7							7
8							8
9							9
10							10
11							11

GENERAL JOURNAL

PAGE _____

	DATE		DESCRIPTION	POST. REF.	DEBIT	CREDIT	
1							1
2							2
3							3
4							4
5							5
6							6
7							7
8							8
9							9
10							10
11							11
12							12
13							13
14							14
15							15
16							16
17							17
18							18

PROBLEM 6.2A or 6.2B (continued)

GENERAL LEDGER

ACCOUNT __Supplies__   ACCOUNT NO. ___121___

DATE	DESCRIPTION	POST. REF.	DEBIT	CREDIT	BALANCE DEBIT	BALANCE CREDIT

ACCOUNT __Prepaid Advertising__   ACCOUNT NO. ___131___

DATE	DESCRIPTION	POST. REF.	DEBIT	CREDIT	BALANCE DEBIT	BALANCE CREDIT

ACCOUNT __Accumulated Depreciation—Equipment__   ACCOUNT NO. ___142___

DATE	DESCRIPTION	POST. REF.	DEBIT	CREDIT	BALANCE DEBIT	BALANCE CREDIT

ACCOUNT __Capital__   ACCOUNT NO. ___301___

DATE	DESCRIPTION	POST. REF.	DEBIT	CREDIT	BALANCE DEBIT	BALANCE CREDIT

ACCOUNT __Drawing__   ACCOUNT NO. ___302___

DATE	DESCRIPTION	POST. REF.	DEBIT	CREDIT	BALANCE DEBIT	BALANCE CREDIT

PROBLEM 6.2A or 6.2B (continued)

GENERAL LEDGER

ACCOUNT __Income Summary__   ACCOUNT NO. ___399___

DATE	DESCRIPTION	POST. REF.	DEBIT	CREDIT	BALANCE DEBIT	CREDIT

ACCOUNT __Fees Income__   ACCOUNT NO. ___401___

DATE	DESCRIPTION	POST. REF.	DEBIT	CREDIT	BALANCE DEBIT	CREDIT

GENERAL LEDGER

ACCOUNT __Salaries Expense__   ACCOUNT NO. ___511___

DATE	DESCRIPTION	POST. REF.	DEBIT	CREDIT	BALANCE DEBIT	CREDIT

ACCOUNT __Utilities Expense__   ACCOUNT NO. ___514___

DATE	DESCRIPTION	POST. REF.	DEBIT	CREDIT	BALANCE DEBIT	CREDIT

ACCOUNT __Supplies Expense__   ACCOUNT NO. ___517___

DATE	DESCRIPTION	POST. REF.	DEBIT	CREDIT	BALANCE DEBIT	CREDIT

PROBLEM 6.2A or 6.2B (continued)

ACCOUNT __Depreciation Expense—Equipment__   ACCOUNT NO. ___523___

DATE	DESCRIPTION	POST. REF.	DEBIT	CREDIT	BALANCE DEBIT	BALANCE CREDIT

ACCOUNT __Advertising Expense__   ACCOUNT NO. ___526___

DATE	DESCRIPTION	POST. REF.	DEBIT	CREDIT	BALANCE DEBIT	BALANCE CREDIT

ACCOUNT NAME	DEBIT	CREDIT

Analyze: _____

PROBLEM 6.3A or 6.3B

GENERAL JOURNAL

	DATE		DESCRIPTION	POST. REF.	DEBIT	CREDIT	
1							1
2							2
3							3
4							4
5							5
6							6
7							7
8							8
9							9
10							10
11							11
12							12
13							13
14							14
15							15
16							16
17							17
18							18
19							19
20							20
21							21
22							22
23							23
24							24
25							25
26							26
27							27
28							28
29							29
30							30
31							31
32							32
33							33
34							34
35							35
36							36
37							37

PROBLEM 6.3A or 6.3B (continued)

GENERAL LEDGER

ACCOUNT _____ **Capital** _____ ACCOUNT NO. ____ **301** ____

DATE	DESCRIPTION	POST. REF.	DEBIT	CREDIT	BALANCE	
					DEBIT	CREDIT

ACCOUNT _____ **Drawing** _____ ACCOUNT NO. ____ **302** ____

DATE	DESCRIPTION	POST. REF.	DEBIT	CREDIT	BALANCE	
					DEBIT	CREDIT

ACCOUNT **Income Summary** _____ ACCOUNT NO. ____ **399** ____

DATE	DESCRIPTION	POST. REF.	DEBIT	CREDIT	BALANCE	
					DEBIT	CREDIT

ACCOUNT **Fees Income** _____ ACCOUNT NO. ____ **401** ____

DATE	DESCRIPTION	POST. REF.	DEBIT	CREDIT	BALANCE	
					DEBIT	CREDIT

Name _____

PROBLEM 6.3A or 6.3B (continued)

GENERAL LEDGER

ACCOUNT __Advertising Expense__   ACCOUNT NO. __511__

DATE	DESCRIPTION	POST. REF.	DEBIT	CREDIT	BALANCE DEBIT	BALANCE CREDIT

ACCOUNT __Depreciation Expense—Equipment__   ACCOUNT NO. __514__

DATE	DESCRIPTION	POST. REF.	DEBIT	CREDIT	BALANCE DEBIT	BALANCE CREDIT

ACCOUNT __Rent Expense__   ACCOUNT NO. __517__

DATE	DESCRIPTION	POST. REF.	DEBIT	CREDIT	BALANCE DEBIT	BALANCE CREDIT

ACCOUNT __Salaries Expense__   ACCOUNT NO. __519__

DATE	DESCRIPTION	POST. REF.	DEBIT	CREDIT	BALANCE DEBIT	BALANCE CREDIT

ACCOUNT __Utilities Expense__   ACCOUNT NO. __523__

DATE	DESCRIPTION	POST. REF.	DEBIT	CREDIT	BALANCE DEBIT	BALANCE CREDIT

Analyze: _____

PROBLEM 6.3A or 6.3B (continued)

GENERAL LEDGER

ACCOUNT _____   ACCOUNT NO. _____

DATE	DESCRIPTION	POST. REF.	DEBIT	CREDIT	BALANCE	
					DEBIT	CREDIT

ACCOUNT _____   ACCOUNT NO. _____

DATE	DESCRIPTION	POST. REF.	DEBIT	CREDIT	BALANCE	
					DEBIT	CREDIT

ACCOUNT _____   ACCOUNT NO. _____

DATE	DESCRIPTION	POST. REF.	DEBIT	CREDIT	BALANCE	
					DEBIT	CREDIT

ACCOUNT _____   ACCOUNT NO. _____

DATE	DESCRIPTION	POST. REF.	DEBIT	CREDIT	BALANCE	
					DEBIT	CREDIT

ACCOUNT _____   ACCOUNT NO. _____

DATE	DESCRIPTION	POST. REF.	DEBIT	CREDIT	BALANCE	
					DEBIT	CREDIT

PROBLEM 6.3A or 6.3B (continued)

GENERAL LEDGER

ACCOUNT _____ ACCOUNT NO. _____

DATE	DESCRIPTION	POST. REF.	DEBIT	CREDIT	BALANCE	
					DEBIT	CREDIT

ACCOUNT _____ ACCOUNT NO. _____

DATE	DESCRIPTION	POST. REF.	DEBIT	CREDIT	BALANCE	
					DEBIT	CREDIT

ACCOUNT _____ ACCOUNT NO. _____

DATE	DESCRIPTION	POST. REF.	DEBIT	CREDIT	BALANCE	
					DEBIT	CREDIT

ACCOUNT _____ ACCOUNT NO. _____

DATE	DESCRIPTION	POST. REF.	DEBIT	CREDIT	BALANCE	
					DEBIT	CREDIT

ACCOUNT _____ ACCOUNT NO. _____

DATE	DESCRIPTION	POST. REF.	DEBIT	CREDIT	BALANCE	
					DEBIT	CREDIT

PROBLEM 6.4A or 6.4B

	ACCOUNT NAME	TRIAL BALANCE		ADJUSTMENTS	
		DEBIT	CREDIT	DEBIT	CREDIT
1					
2					
3					
4					
5					
6					
7					
8					
9					
10					
11					
12					
13					
14					
15					
16					
17					
18					
19					
20					
21					
22					
23					
24					
25					
26					
27					
28					
29					
30					
31					
32					

PROBLEM 6.4A or 6.4B (continued)

ADJUSTED TRIAL BALANCE		INCOME STATEMENT		BALANCE SHEET		
DEBIT	CREDIT	DEBIT	CREDIT	DEBIT	CREDIT	
						1
						2
						3
						4
						5
						6
						7
						8
						9
						10
						11
						12
						13
						14
						15
						16
						17
						18
						19
						20
						21
						22
						23
						24
						25
						26
						27
						28
						29
						30
						31
						32

PROBLEM 6.4A or 6.4B (continued)

GENERAL JOURNAL

PAGE _____

	DATE		DESCRIPTION	POST. REF.	DEBIT	CREDIT	
1							1
2							2
3							3
4							4
5							5
6							6
7							7
8							8
9							9
10							10
11							11
12							12
13							13

GENERAL JOURNAL

PAGE _____

	DATE		DESCRIPTION	POST. REF.	DEBIT	CREDIT	
1							1
2							2
3							3
4							4
5							5
6							6
7							7
8							8
9							9
10							10
11							11
12							12
13							13
14							14
15							15
16							16
17							17
18							18

PROBLEM 6.4A or 6.4B (continued)

GENERAL LEDGER

ACCOUNT **Supplies**   ACCOUNT NO. **121**

DATE	DESCRIPTION	POST. REF.	DEBIT	CREDIT	BALANCE DEBIT	BALANCE CREDIT

ACCOUNT **Prepaid Advertising**   ACCOUNT NO. **131**

DATE	DESCRIPTION	POST. REF.	DEBIT	CREDIT	BALANCE DEBIT	BALANCE CREDIT

ACCOUNT **Accumulated Depreciation—**   ACCOUNT NO. **142**

DATE	DESCRIPTION	POST. REF.	DEBIT	CREDIT	BALANCE DEBIT	BALANCE CREDIT

ACCOUNT **Capital**   ACCOUNT NO. **301**

DATE	DESCRIPTION	POST. REF.	DEBIT	CREDIT	BALANCE DEBIT	BALANCE CREDIT

ACCOUNT **Drawing**   ACCOUNT NO. **302**

DATE	DESCRIPTION	POST. REF.	DEBIT	CREDIT	BALANCE DEBIT	BALANCE CREDIT

PROBLEM 6.4A or 6.4B (continued)

GENERAL LEDGER

ACCOUNT __Income Summary__   ACCOUNT NO. __399__

DATE		DESCRIPTION	POST. REF.	DEBIT	CREDIT	BALANCE DEBIT	BALANCE CREDIT

ACCOUNT __Fees Income__   ACCOUNT NO. __401__

DATE		DESCRIPTION	POST. REF.	DEBIT	CREDIT	BALANCE DEBIT	BALANCE CREDIT

GENERAL LEDGER

ACCOUNT __Salaries Expense__   ACCOUNT NO. __511__

DATE		DESCRIPTION	POST. REF.	DEBIT	CREDIT	BALANCE DEBIT	BALANCE CREDIT

ACCOUNT __Utilities Expense__   ACCOUNT NO. __514__

DATE		DESCRIPTION	POST. REF.	DEBIT	CREDIT	BALANCE DEBIT	BALANCE CREDIT

ACCOUNT __Supplies Expense__   ACCOUNT NO. __517__

DATE		DESCRIPTION	POST. REF.	DEBIT	CREDIT	BALANCE DEBIT	BALANCE CREDIT

PROBLEM 6.4A or 6.4B (continued)

ACCOUNT __Depreciation Expense—_____ ACCOUNT NO. ___523___

DATE	DESCRIPTION	POST. REF.	DEBIT	CREDIT	BALANCE	
					DEBIT	CREDIT

ACCOUNT __Advertising Expense_____ ACCOUNT NO. ___526___

DATE	DESCRIPTION	POST. REF.	DEBIT	CREDIT	BALANCE	
					DEBIT	CREDIT

ACCOUNT NAME	DEBIT	CREDIT

Analyze: _____
_____

CRITICAL THINKING PROBLEM 6.1

21st Century Fashions

Worksheet

Month Ended December 31, 2016

	ACCOUNT NAME	TRIAL BALANCE DEBIT	TRIAL BALANCE CREDIT	ADJUSTMENTS DEBIT	ADJUSTMENTS CREDIT
1	Cash	81 6 0 0 00			
2	Accounts Receivable	18 0 0 0 00			
3	Supplies	14 4 0 0 00			(a) 7 2 0 0 00
4	Prepaid Insurance	21 6 0 0 00			(b) 4 8 0 0 00
5	Machinery	168 0 0 0 00			
6	Accumulated Depreciation—Machinery				(c) 2 4 0 0 00
7	Accounts Payable		27 0 0 0 00		
8	Carolyn Davis, Capital		149 1 6 0 00		
9	Carolyn Davis, Drawing	12 0 0 0 00			
10	Fees Income		165 0 0 0 00		
11	Supplies Expense			(a) 7 2 0 0 00	
12	Insurance Expense			(b) 4 8 0 0 00	
13	Salaries Expense	22 2 0 0 00			
14	Depreciation Expense—Machinery			(c) 2 4 0 0 00	
15	Utilities Expense	3 3 6 0 00			
16	Totals	341 1 6 0 00	341 1 6 0 00	14 4 0 0 00	14 4 0 0 00
17	Net Income				
18					
19					
20					
21					
22					
23					
24					
25					
26					
27					
28					
29					
30					
31					
32					

CRITICAL THINKING PROBLEM 6.1 (continued)

_____

_____

	ADJUSTED TRIAL BALANCE		INCOME STATEMENT		BALANCE SHEET		
	DEBIT	CREDIT	DEBIT	CREDIT	DEBIT	CREDIT	
1							1
2							2
3							3
4							4
5							5
6							6
7							7
8							8
9							9
10							10
11							11
12							12
13							13
14							14
15							15
16							16
17							17
18							18
19							19
20							20
21							21
22							22
23							23
24							24
25							25
26							26
27							27
28							28
29							29
30							30
31							31
32							32

CRITICAL THINKING PROBLEM 6.1 (continued)

CRITICAL THINKING PROBLEM 6.1 (continued)

_____
_____

GENERAL JOURNAL

PAGE _____

	DATE	DESCRIPTION	POST. REF.	DEBIT	CREDIT	
1						1
2						2
3						3
4						4
5						5
6						6
7						7
8						8
9						9
10						10
11						11
12						12
13						13
14						14
15						15
16						16

CRITICAL THINKING PROBLEM 6.1 (continued)

GENERAL JOURNAL

PAGE _____

	DATE	DESCRIPTION	POST. REF.	DEBIT	CREDIT	
1						1
2						2
3						3
4						4
5						5
6						6
7						7
8						8
9						9
10						10
11						11
12						12
13						13
14						14
15						15
16						16
17						17
18						18

	ACCOUNT NAME	DEBIT	CREDIT

Analyze: _____

_____

CRITICAL THINKING PROBLEM 6.2

1. _____

_____

_____

_____

_____

_____

_____

_____

_____

2.

GENERAL JOURNAL   PAGE _____

	DATE		DESCRIPTION	POST. REF.	DEBIT	CREDIT	
1							1
2							2
3							3
4							4
5							5
6							6

3. _____

_____

_____

_____

_____

_____

_____

_____

_____

_____

_____

_____

_____

_____

CRITICAL THINKING PROBLEM 6.2 (continued)

_____
_____
_____
_____
_____
_____
_____
_____
_____
_____
_____
_____
_____
_____
_____
_____
_____
_____
_____
_____

Chapter 6 Practice Test Answer Key

Part A True-False	Part B Matching
1. F	1. d
2. T	2. c
3. F	3. e
4. T	4. b
5. F	5. a
6. F	
7. T	
8. F	
9. F	
10. T	

MINI-PRACTICE SET 1

Service Business Accounting Cycle

GENERAL JOURNAL

PAGE _____

	DATE	DESCRIPTION	POST. REF.	DEBIT	CREDIT	
1						1
2						2
3						3
4						4
5						5
6						6
7						7
8						8
9						9
10						10
11						11
12						12
13						13
14						14
15						15
16						16
17						17
18						18
19						19
20						20
21						21
22						22
23						23
24						24
25						25
26						26
27						27
28						28
29						29
30						30
31						31
32						32
33						33
34						34

Name _____

GENERAL JOURNAL   PAGE _____

	DATE	DESCRIPTION	POST. REF.	DEBIT	CREDIT	
1						1
2						2
3						3
4						4
5						5
6						6
7						7
8						8
9						9
10						10
11						11
12						12
13						13
14						14
15						15
16						16
17						17
18						18
19						19
20						20
21						21
22						22
23						23
24						24
25						25
26						26
27						27
28						28
29						29
30						30
31						31
32						32
33						33
34						34
35						35
36						36
37						37
38						38
39						39

Name _____

GENERAL JOURNAL

PAGE _____

	DATE		DESCRIPTION	POST. REF.	DEBIT	CREDIT	
1							1
2							2
3							3
4							4
5							5
6							6
7							7
8							8
9							9
10							10
11							11
12							12
13							13
14							14
15							15
16							16
17							17
18							18
19							19
20							20
21							21
22							22
23							23
24							24
25							25
26							26
27							27
28							28
29							29
30							30
31							31
32							32
33							33
34							34
35							35
36							36
37							37
38							38
39							39

Name _____

GENERAL JOURNAL

PAGE _____

	DATE		DESCRIPTION	POST. REF.	DEBIT	CREDIT	
1							1
2							2
3							3
4							4
5							5
6							6
7							7
8							8
9							9
10							10
11							11
12							12
13							13
14							14
15							15
16							16
17							17
18							18
19							19
20							20
21							21
22							22
23							23
24							24
25							25
26							26
27							27
28							28
29							29
30							30
31							31
32							32
33							33
34							34
35							35
36							36
37							37
38							38
39							39

GENERAL LEDGER

ACCOUNT _____   ACCOUNT NO. _____

DATE	DESCRIPTION	POST. REF.	DEBIT	CREDIT	BALANCE	
					DEBIT	CREDIT

ACCOUNT _____   ACCOUNT NO. _____

DATE	DESCRIPTION	POST. REF.	DEBIT	CREDIT	BALANCE	
					DEBIT	CREDIT

Name _____

GENERAL LEDGER

ACCOUNT _____ ACCOUNT NO. _____

DATE	DESCRIPTION	POST. REF.	DEBIT	CREDIT	BALANCE	
					DEBIT	CREDIT

ACCOUNT _____ ACCOUNT NO. _____

DATE	DESCRIPTION	POST. REF.	DEBIT	CREDIT	BALANCE	
					DEBIT	CREDIT

ACCOUNT _____ ACCOUNT NO. _____

DATE	DESCRIPTION	POST. REF.	DEBIT	CREDIT	BALANCE	
					DEBIT	CREDIT

ACCOUNT _____ ACCOUNT NO. _____

DATE	DESCRIPTION	POST. REF.	DEBIT	CREDIT	BALANCE	
					DEBIT	CREDIT

ACCOUNT _____ ACCOUNT NO. _____

DATE	DESCRIPTION	POST. REF.	DEBIT	CREDIT	BALANCE	
					DEBIT	CREDIT

GENERAL LEDGER

ACCOUNT _____   ACCOUNT NO. _____

	DATE	DESCRIPTION	POST. REF.	DEBIT	CREDIT	BALANCE	
						DEBIT	CREDIT

ACCOUNT _____   ACCOUNT NO. _____

	DATE	DESCRIPTION	POST. REF.	DEBIT	CREDIT	BALANCE	
						DEBIT	CREDIT

ACCOUNT _____   ACCOUNT NO. _____

	DATE	DESCRIPTION	POST. REF.	DEBIT	CREDIT	BALANCE	
						DEBIT	CREDIT

ACCOUNT _____   ACCOUNT NO. _____

	DATE	DESCRIPTION	POST. REF.	DEBIT	CREDIT	BALANCE	
						DEBIT	CREDIT

Name _____

GENERAL LEDGER

ACCOUNT _____ ACCOUNT NO. _____

	DATE	DESCRIPTION	POST. REF.	DEBIT	CREDIT	BALANCE	
						DEBIT	CREDIT

ACCOUNT _____ ACCOUNT NO. _____

	DATE	DESCRIPTION	POST. REF.	DEBIT	CREDIT	BALANCE	
						DEBIT	CREDIT

ACCOUNT _____ ACCOUNT NO. _____

	DATE	DESCRIPTION	POST. REF.	DEBIT	CREDIT	BALANCE	
						DEBIT	CREDIT

ACCOUNT _____ ACCOUNT NO. _____

	DATE	DESCRIPTION	POST. REF.	DEBIT	CREDIT	BALANCE	
						DEBIT	CREDIT

ACCOUNT _____ ACCOUNT NO. _____

	DATE	DESCRIPTION	POST. REF.	DEBIT	CREDIT	BALANCE	
						DEBIT	CREDIT

GENERAL LEDGER

ACCOUNT _____   ACCOUNT NO. _____

DATE	DESCRIPTION	POST. REF.	DEBIT	CREDIT	BALANCE DEBIT	CREDIT

ACCOUNT _____   ACCOUNT NO. _____

DATE	DESCRIPTION	POST. REF.	DEBIT	CREDIT	BALANCE DEBIT	CREDIT

ACCOUNT _____   ACCOUNT NO. _____

DATE	DESCRIPTION	POST. REF.	DEBIT	CREDIT	BALANCE DEBIT	CREDIT

ACCOUNT _____   ACCOUNT NO. _____

DATE	DESCRIPTION	POST. REF.	DEBIT	CREDIT	BALANCE DEBIT	CREDIT

ACCOUNT _____   ACCOUNT NO. _____

DATE	DESCRIPTION	POST. REF.	DEBIT	CREDIT	BALANCE DEBIT	CREDIT

	ACCOUNT NAME	TRIAL BALANCE		ADJUSTMENTS	
		DEBIT	CREDIT	DEBIT	CREDIT
1					
2					
3					
4					
5					
6					
7					
8					
9					
10					
11					
12					
13					
14					
15					
16					
17					
18					
19					
20					
21					
22					
23					
24					
25					
26					
27					
28					
29					
30					
31					
32					
33					
34					
35					
36					
37					

_____

_____

	ADJUSTED TRIAL BALANCE		INCOME STATEMENT		BALANCE SHEET		
	DEBIT	CREDIT	DEBIT	CREDIT	DEBIT	CREDIT	
							1
							2
							3
							4
							5
							6
							7
							8
							9
							10
							11
							12
							13
							14
							15
							16
							17
							18
							19
							20
							21
							22
							23
							24
							25
							26
							27
							28
							29
							30
							31
							32
							33
							34
							35
							36
							37

Name

_____

_____

ACCOUNT NAME	DEBIT	CREDIT	

MINI-PRACTICE SET 1 (continued)

Analyze: _____

CHAPTER 7

Accounting for Sales and Accounts Receivable

STUDY GUIDE

Understanding the Chapter

Objectives	**1.** Record credit sales in a sales journal. **2.** Post from the sales journal to the general ledger accounts. **3.** Post from the sales journal to the customers' accounts in the accounts receivable subsidiary ledger. **4.** Record sales returns and allowances in the general journal. **5.** Post sales returns and allowances. **6.** Prepare a schedule of accounts receivable. **7.** Compute trade discounts. **8.** Record credit card sales in appropriate journals. **9.** Prepare the state sales tax return. **10.** Define the accounting terms new to this chapter.
Reading Assignment	Read Chapter 7 in the textbook. Complete the textbook Section Self Review as you finish reading each section of the chapter, and the Comprehensive Self Review at the end of the chapter. Refer to the Chapter 7 Glossary or to the Glossary at the end of the book to find definitions for terms that are not familiar to you.

Activities

❏ **Thinking Critically**	Answer the *Thinking Critically* questions for Kellogg's and Managerial Implications.
❏ **Discussion Questions**	Answer each assigned discussion question in Chapter 7.
❏ **Exercises**	Complete each assigned exercise in Chapter 7. Use the forms provided in this SGWP. The objectives covered by an exercise are given after the exercise number. If you need help with an exercise, review the portion of the chapter related to the objective(s) covered.
❏ **Problems A/B**	Complete each assigned problem in Chapter 7. Use the forms provided in this SGWP. The objectives covered by a problem are given after the problem number. If you need help with a problem, review the portion of the chapter related to the objective(s) covered.
❏ **Critical Thinking Problems**	Complete the critical thinking problems 7.1 and 7.2 as assigned. Use the forms provided in this SGWP.
❏ **Business Connections**	Complete the Business Connections activities as assigned to gain a deeper understanding of Chapter 7 concepts.

Practice Tests

Complete the Practice Tests, which cover the main points in your reading assignment. Compare your answers with those in the Practice Test Answer Key for Chapter 7 at the end of this chapter. If you have answered any questions incorrectly, review the related section of the text.

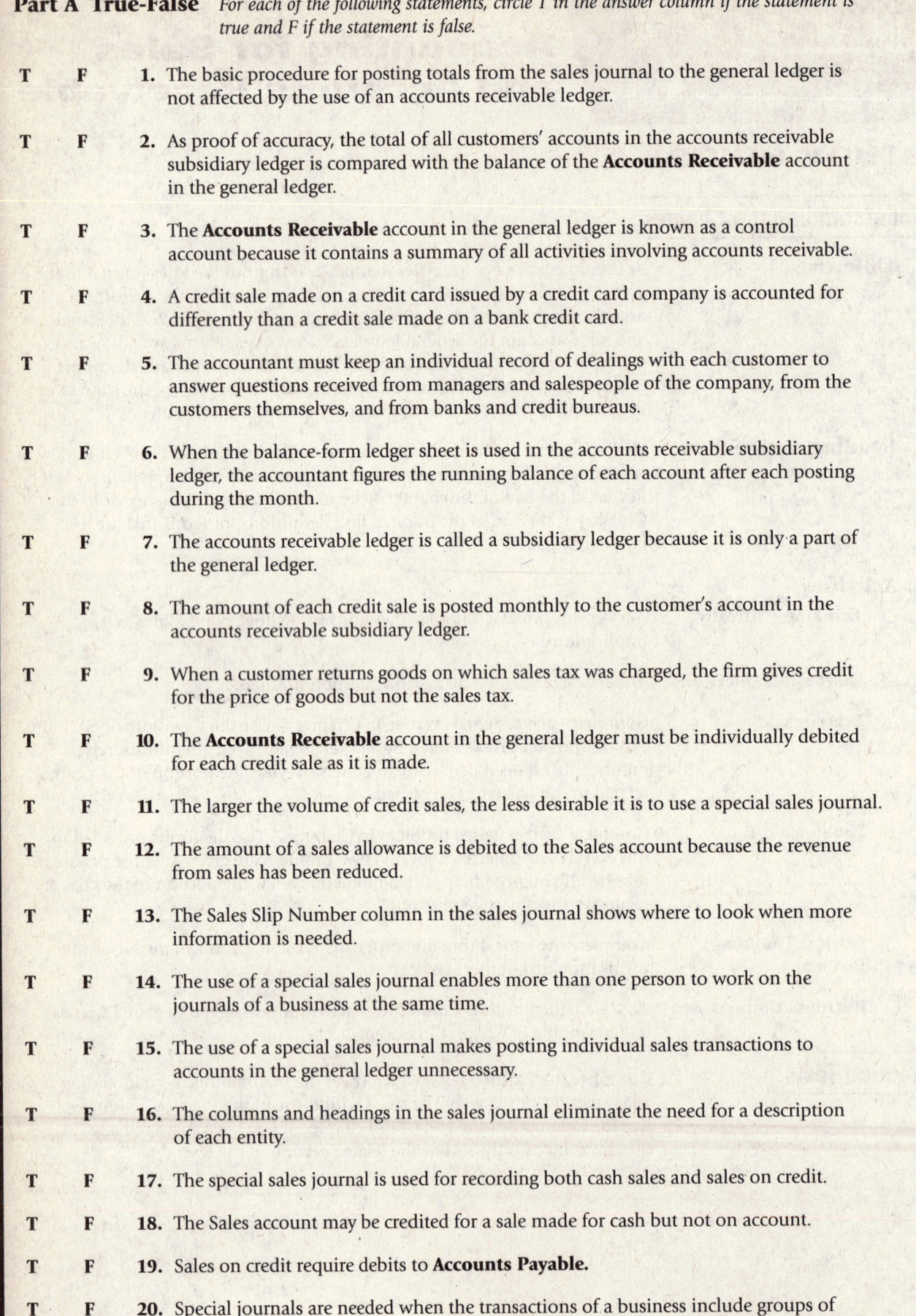

Part A True-False *For each of the following statements, circle T in the answer column if the statement is true and F if the statement is false.*

T   F   **1.** The basic procedure for posting totals from the sales journal to the general ledger is not affected by the use of an accounts receivable ledger.

T   F   **2.** As proof of accuracy, the total of all customers' accounts in the accounts receivable subsidiary ledger is compared with the balance of the **Accounts Receivable** account in the general ledger.

T   F   **3.** The **Accounts Receivable** account in the general ledger is known as a control account because it contains a summary of all activities involving accounts receivable.

T   F   **4.** A credit sale made on a credit card issued by a credit card company is accounted for differently than a credit sale made on a bank credit card.

T   F   **5.** The accountant must keep an individual record of dealings with each customer to answer questions received from managers and salespeople of the company, from the customers themselves, and from banks and credit bureaus.

T   F   **6.** When the balance-form ledger sheet is used in the accounts receivable subsidiary ledger, the accountant figures the running balance of each account after each posting during the month.

T   F   **7.** The accounts receivable ledger is called a subsidiary ledger because it is only a part of the general ledger.

T   F   **8.** The amount of each credit sale is posted monthly to the customer's account in the accounts receivable subsidiary ledger.

T   F   **9.** When a customer returns goods on which sales tax was charged, the firm gives credit for the price of goods but not the sales tax.

T   F   **10.** The **Accounts Receivable** account in the general ledger must be individually debited for each credit sale as it is made.

T   F   **11.** The larger the volume of credit sales, the less desirable it is to use a special sales journal.

T   F   **12.** The amount of a sales allowance is debited to the Sales account because the revenue from sales has been reduced.

T   F   **13.** The Sales Slip Number column in the sales journal shows where to look when more information is needed.

T   F   **14.** The use of a special sales journal enables more than one person to work on the journals of a business at the same time.

T   F   **15.** The use of a special sales journal makes posting individual sales transactions to accounts in the general ledger unnecessary.

T   F   **16.** The columns and headings in the sales journal eliminate the need for a description of each entity.

T   F   **17.** The special sales journal is used for recording both cash sales and sales on credit.

T   F   **18.** The Sales account may be credited for a sale made for cash but not on account.

T   F   **19.** Sales on credit require debits to **Accounts Payable.**

T   F   **20.** Special journals are needed when the transactions of a business include groups of repetitive entries.

Part B Matching *For each numbered item, choose the matching term from the box and write the identifying letter in the answer column.*

_____ 1. A reduction in the amount charged to a customer who has received defective goods or services.

_____ 2. A special journal for recording only the credit sales of a company.

_____ 3. A liability account for recording a tax levied by some states on certain retail sales.

_____ 4. Identification cards used by some banks to individuals for use in making credit card purchases at participating businesses.

_____ 5. Identification cards given by some businesses to their customers who have established credit.

_____ 6. A reduction in price, based on volume purchased, given by wholesalers to retailers who buy goods for resale.

_____ 7. The type of credit usually given by a business on the basis of the personal knowledge of the customer.

> a. Trade discount
> b. Sales return or allowance
> c. Business credit card
> d. Sales tax payable
> e. Open-account credit
> f. Sales journal
> g. Bank credit cards

Part C Exercise *Answer each question about the accounts receivable subsidiary ledger account shown below.*

ACCOUNTS RECEIVABLE SUBSIDIARY LEDGER

NAME __Chris Stamos_____ TERMS _____

ADDRESS __1891 Windsor Drive, Dallas, TX 75623-6998_____

DATE		DESCRIPTION	POST. REF.	DEBIT	CREDIT	BALANCE DEBIT	BALANCE CREDIT
2016							
Jan.	1	Balance	✔			4 0 0 00	
	4	Sales Slip 101	S1	9 0 00		4 9 0 00	
	7	Sales Slip 167	S1	9 0 00		5 8 0 00	
	18		J1		5 0 00	5 3 0 00	

1. Where did the $400 entry come from?

_____

_____

2. How could you find a complete description of the $90 charge on January 4?

_____

_____

3. What was the probable reason for the $50.00 entry on January 18? How can you find out for sure?

_____

_____

Demonstration Problem

SoCal Auto Supply sells tires and auto supplies to retail stores. Transactions involving credit sales and sales returns and allowances for the month of April 2016 follow, along with the general ledger accounts used to record these transactions. Account balances shown are for the beginning of April 2016.

Instructions

1. Open the general ledger accounts; enter the balance for **Accounts Receivable.**

    111   Accounts Receivable $61,020
    401   Sales
    451   Sales Returns and Allowances

2. Set up the accounts receivable subsidiary ledger. Open an account for each credit customer and enter the balances as of April 1, 2016. All customers have terms of n/45.

Auto Warehouse	$ —
Danny's Auto Mart	$14,790
Jazzy Wheels and Window Tint Center	$42,000
Mike's Car Care Center	$4,230
Saratoga Auto	$ —

3. Record the transactions on page 6 of a sales journal and on page 16 of the general journal. (Be sure to enter each sale at its net price.)

4. Post individual entries from the sales journal and the general journal to the appropriate ledger accounts.

5. Total and rule the sales journal as of April 30, 2016.

6. Post from the sales journal to the appropriate general ledger accounts.

7. Prepare a schedule of accounts receivable for April 30, 2016.

8. Compare the total of the schedule of accounts receivable to the balance of the **Accounts Receivable** account. The two should be equal.

DATE	TRANSACTIONS
April 1	Sold tires to Auto Warehouse; issued sales slip 6701 with a list price of $52,000.
5	Sold auto supplies to Mike's Car Care Center; issued sales slip 6702 with a list price of $50,200.
9	Sold auto supplies to Jazzy Wheels and Window Tint Center; issued sales slip 6703 with a list price of $19,800.
14	Sold tires to Danny's Auto Mart, issued sales slip 6704 with a list price of $47,200.
18	Accepted a return of all auto supplies damaged in shipment to Jazzy Wheels and Window Tint Center; issued Credit Memorandum 251. The original sale was made on sales slip 6703 on April 9.
22	Sold auto supplies to Auto Warehouse; issued sales slip 6705 with a list price of $63,480.
29	Sold tires to Mike's Car Care Center; issued sales slip 6706 with a list price of $87,230.
30	Sold tires to Saratoga Auto; issued sales slip 6707 with a list price of $45,320.

SOLUTION

SALES JOURNAL

	DATE		INVOICE NO.	CUSTOMER'S NAME	POST. REF.	ACCOUNTS RECEIVABLE/ DR. SALES CR.	
1	2016						1
2	April	1	6701	Auto Warehouse	✔	52 0 0 0 00	2
3		5	6702	Mike's Car Care Center	✔	50 2 0 0 00	3
4		9	6703	Jazzy Wheels and Window Tint Center	✔	19 8 0 0 00	4
5		14	6704	Danny's Auto Mart	✔	47 2 0 0 00	5
6		22	6705	Auto Warehouse	✔	63 4 8 0 00	6
7		29	6706	Mike's Car Care Center	✔	87 2 3 0 00	7
8		30	6707	Saratoga Auto	✔	45 3 2 0 00	8
9				Totals		365 2 3 0 00	9
10						(1 1 1/4 01)	10
11							11

GENERAL JOURNAL

	DATE		DESCRIPTION	POST. REF.	DEBIT	CREDIT	
1	2016						1
2	April	18	Sales Returns and Allowances	451	19 8 0 0 00		2
3			Accounts Rec./Jazzy Wheels	111 ✔		19 8 0 0 00	3
4			and Window Tint Center				4
5			Accepted return of damaged supplies,				5
6			Credit Memo 251; original sale				6
7			made on Invoice 6703 of April 9				7
8							8

GENERAL LEDGER

ACCOUNT __Accounts Receivable__   ACCOUNT NO. ____111____

DATE		DESCRIPTION	POST. REF.	DEBIT	CREDIT	BALANCE DEBIT	BALANCE CREDIT
2016							
April	1	Balance	✔			61 0 2 0 00	
	18		J16		19 8 0 0 00	41 2 2 0 00	
	30		S6	365 2 3 0 00		406 4 5 0 00	

SOLUTION (continued)

GENERAL LEDGER

ACCOUNT Sales   **ACCOUNT NO.** 401

DATE		DESCRIPTION	POST. REF.	DEBIT	CREDIT	BALANCE DEBIT	BALANCE CREDIT
2016							
April	30		S6		365 2 3 0 00		365 2 3 0 00

ACCOUNT Sales Returns and Allowances   **ACCOUNT NO.** 451

DATE		DESCRIPTION	POST. REF.	DEBIT	CREDIT	BALANCE DEBIT	BALANCE CREDIT
2016							
April	18		J16	19 8 0 0 00		19 8 0 0 00	

ACCOUNTS RECEIVABLE SUBSIDIARY LEDGER

NAME Auto Warehouse   **TERMS** n/45

DATE		DESCRIPTION	POST. REF.	DEBIT	CREDIT	BALANCE DEBIT	BALANCE CREDIT
2016							
April	1	Sales Slip 6701	S6	52 0 0 0 00		52 0 0 0 00	
	22	Sales Slip 6705	S6	63 4 8 0 00		115 4 8 0 00	

NAME Danny's Auto Mart   **TERMS** n/45

DATE		DESCRIPTION	POST. REF.	DEBIT	CREDIT	BALANCE DEBIT	BALANCE CREDIT
2016							
April	1	Balance	✔			14 7 9 0 00	
	14	Sales Slip 6704	S6	47 2 0 0 00		61 9 9 0 00	

SOLUTION (continued)

ACCOUNTS RECEIVABLE SUBSIDIARY LEDGER

NAME ___Jazzy Wheels and Window Tint Center_____ TERMS ___n/45___

DATE		DESCRIPTION	POST. REF.	DEBIT	CREDIT	BALANCE DEBIT	BALANCE CREDIT
2016							
April	1	Balance	✔			42 0 0 0 00	
	9	Sales Slip 6703	S6	19 8 0 0 00		61 8 0 0 00	
	18	CM 251	J16		19 8 0 0 00	42 0 0 0 00	

NAME ___Mike's Car Care Center_____ TERMS ___n/45___

DATE		DESCRIPTION	POST. REF.	DEBIT	CREDIT	BALANCE DEBIT	BALANCE CREDIT
2016							
April	1	Balance	✔			4 2 3 0 00	
	5	Sales Slip 6702	S6	50 2 0 0 00		54 4 3 0 00	
	29	Sales Slip 6706	S6	87 2 3 0 00		141 6 6 0 00	

NAME ___Saratoga Auto_____ TERMS ___n/45___

DATE		DESCRIPTION	POST. REF.	DEBIT	CREDIT	BALANCE DEBIT	BALANCE CREDIT
2016							
April	30	Sales Slip 6707	S6	45 3 2 0 00		45 3 2 0 00	

SoCal Auto Supply

Schedule of Accounts Receivable

April 30, 2016

Auto Warehouse	115 4 8 0 00
Danny's Auto Mart	61 9 9 0 00
Jazzy Wheels and Window Tint Center	42 0 0 0 00
Mike's Car Care Center	141 6 6 0 00
Saratoga Auto	45 3 2 0 00
Total	406 4 5 0 00

WORKING PAPERS

Name _____

EXERCISE 7.1

1. _____   5. _____
2. _____   6. _____
3. _____   7. _____
4. _____   8. _____

EXERCISE 7.2

	Dr.	Cr.		Dr.	Cr.
1.	_____	_____	4.	_____	_____
2.	_____	_____	5.	_____	_____
3.	_____	_____	6.	_____	_____

EXERCISE 7.3

SALES JOURNAL   PAGE _____

	DATE	SALES SLIP NO.	CUSTOMER'S NAME	POST. REF.	ACCOUNTS RECEIVABLE DEBIT	SALES TAX PAYABLE CREDIT	SALES CREDIT	
1								1
2								2
3								3
4								4
5								5

EXERCISE 7.4

GENERAL JOURNAL

PAGE _____

	DATE		DESCRIPTION	POST. REF.	DEBIT	CREDIT	
1							1
2							2
3							3
4							4
5							5
6							6
7							7
8							8
9							9
10							10
11							11
12							12
13							13
14							14
15							15

EXERCISE 7.5

1. _____
_____
_____

2. _____
_____
_____

3. _____
_____
_____

4. _____
_____
_____

EXERCISE 7.6

1. _____
2. _____
3. _____

EXERCISE 7.7

1. _____
2. _____
3. _____

EXERCISE 7.8

GENERAL JOURNAL   PAGE _____

	DATE		DESCRIPTION	POST. REF.	DEBIT	CREDIT	
1							1
2							2
3							3
4							4
5							5

EXERCISE 7.9

_____

Balance of Accounts Receivable: _____

EXERCISE 7.10

GENERAL LEDGER

ACCOUNT _____ ACCOUNT NO. _____

	DATE	DESCRIPTION	POST. REF.	DEBIT	CREDIT	BALANCE	
						DEBIT	CREDIT

ACCOUNT _____ ACCOUNT NO. _____

	DATE	DESCRIPTION	POST. REF.	DEBIT	CREDIT	BALANCE	
						DEBIT	CREDIT

ACCOUNT _____ ACCOUNT NO. _____

	DATE	DESCRIPTION	POST. REF.	DEBIT	CREDIT	BALANCE	
						DEBIT	CREDIT

ACCOUNTS RECEIVABLE SUBSIDIARY LEDGER

NAME _____ TERMS _____

	DATE	DESCRIPTION	POST. REF.	DEBIT	CREDIT	BALANCE

NAME _____ TERMS _____

	DATE	DESCRIPTION	POST. REF.	DEBIT	CREDIT	BALANCE

PROBLEM 7.1A or 7.1B

SALES JOURNAL

PAGE _____

	DATE	SALES SLIP NO.	CUSTOMER'S NAME	POST. REF.	ACCOUNTS RECEIVABLE DEBIT	SALES TAX PAYABLE CREDIT	SALES CREDIT	
1								1
2								2
3								3
4								4
5								5
6								6
7								7
8								8
9								9
10								10
11								11
12								12

GENERAL LEDGER

ACCOUNT _____ ACCOUNT NO. _____

DATE	DESCRIPTION	POST. REF.	DEBIT	CREDIT	BALANCE DEBIT	BALANCE CREDIT

ACCOUNT _____ ACCOUNT NO. _____

DATE	DESCRIPTION	POST. REF.	DEBIT	CREDIT	BALANCE DEBIT	BALANCE CREDIT

ACCOUNT _____ ACCOUNT NO. _____

DATE	DESCRIPTION	POST. REF.	DEBIT	CREDIT	BALANCE DEBIT	BALANCE CREDIT

Analyze: _____

_____

PROBLEM 7.2A or 7.2B

SALES JOURNAL

PAGE _____

	DATE	SALES SLIP NO.	CUSTOMER'S NAME	POST. REF.	ACCOUNTS RECEIVABLE DEBIT	SALES TAX PAYABLE CREDIT	SALES CREDIT	
1								1
2								2
3								3
4								4
5								5
6								6
7								7
8								8
9								9
10								10
11								11
12								12

GENERAL JOURNAL

PAGE _____

	DATE	DESCRIPTION	POST. REF.	DEBIT	CREDIT	
1						1
2						2
3						3
4						4
5						5
6						6
7						7
8						8
9						9
10						10
11						11
12						12
13						13
14						14
15						15
16						16
17						17
18						18
19						19
20						20
21						21

PROBLEM 7.2A or 7.2B (continued)

GENERAL LEDGER

ACCOUNT _____ ACCOUNT NO. _____

DATE		DESCRIPTION	POST. REF.	DEBIT	CREDIT	BALANCE	
						DEBIT	CREDIT

ACCOUNT _____ ACCOUNT NO. _____

DATE		DESCRIPTION	POST. REF.	DEBIT	CREDIT	BALANCE	
						DEBIT	CREDIT

ACCOUNT _____ ACCOUNT NO. _____

DATE		DESCRIPTION	POST. REF.	DEBIT	CREDIT	BALANCE	
						DEBIT	CREDIT

ACCOUNT _____ ACCOUNT NO. _____

DATE		DESCRIPTION	POST. REF.	DEBIT	CREDIT	BALANCE	
						DEBIT	CREDIT

PROBLEM 7.2A or 7.2B (continued)

Analyze: _____

_____

PROBLEM 7.3A or 7.3B

SALES JOURNAL   PAGE _____

	DATE	SALES SLIP NO.	CUSTOMER'S NAME	POST. REF.	ACCOUNTS RECEIVABLE DEBIT	SALES TAX PAYABLE CREDIT	SALES CREDIT	
1								1
2								2
3								3
4								4
5								5
6								6
7								7
8								8
9								9
10								10
11								11
12								12

PROBLEM 7.3A or 7.3B (continued)

GENERAL JOURNAL

PAGE _____

	DATE		DESCRIPTION	POST. REF.	DEBIT	CREDIT	
1							1
2							2
3							3
4							4
5							5
6							6
7							7
8							8
9							9
10							10
11							11
12							12
13							13
14							14
15							15

GENERAL LEDGER

ACCOUNT _____ ACCOUNT NO. _____

DATE	DESCRIPTION	POST. REF.	DEBIT	CREDIT	BALANCE	
					DEBIT	CREDIT

ACCOUNT _____ ACCOUNT NO. _____

DATE	DESCRIPTION	POST. REF.	DEBIT	CREDIT	BALANCE	
					DEBIT	CREDIT

PROBLEM 7.3A or 7.3B (continued)

GENERAL LEDGER

ACCOUNT _____ ACCOUNT NO. _____

	DATE	DESCRIPTION	POST. REF.	DEBIT	CREDIT	BALANCE	
						DEBIT	CREDIT

ACCOUNT _____ ACCOUNT NO. _____

	DATE	DESCRIPTION	POST. REF.	DEBIT	CREDIT	BALANCE	
						DEBIT	CREDIT

ACCOUNTS RECEIVABLE SUBSIDIARY LEDGER

NAME _____ TERMS _____

	DATE	DESCRIPTION	POST. REF.	DEBIT	CREDIT	BALANCE

NAME _____ TERMS _____

	DATE	DESCRIPTION	POST. REF.	DEBIT	CREDIT	BALANCE

NAME _____ TERMS _____

	DATE	DESCRIPTION	POST. REF.	DEBIT	CREDIT	BALANCE

PROBLEM 7.3A or 7.3B (continued)

ACCOUNTS RECEIVABLE SUBSIDIARY LEDGER

NAME _____ TERMS _____

	DATE	DESCRIPTION	POST. REF.	DEBIT	CREDIT	BALANCE

NAME _____ TERMS _____

	DATE	DESCRIPTION	POST. REF.	DEBIT	CREDIT	BALANCE

NAME _____ TERMS _____

	DATE	DESCRIPTION	POST. REF.	DEBIT	CREDIT	BALANCE

NAME _____ TERMS _____

	DATE	DESCRIPTION	POST. REF.	DEBIT	CREDIT	BALANCE

NAME _____ TERMS _____

	DATE	DESCRIPTION	POST. REF.	DEBIT	CREDIT	BALANCE

NAME _____ TERMS _____

	DATE	DESCRIPTION	POST. REF.	DEBIT	CREDIT	BALANCE

Name _____

PROBLEM 7.3A or 7.3B (continued)

Balance of Accounts Receivable account: _____

Analyze: _____
_____

PROBLEM 7.4A or 7.4B

SALES JOURNAL

PAGE _____

	DATE	SALES SLIP NO.	CUSTOMER'S NAME	POST. REF.	ACCOUNTS RECEIVABLE DR./ SALES CR.	
1						1
2						2
3						3
4						4
5						5
6						6
7						7
8						8
9						9
10						10
11						11
12						12

PROBLEM 7.4A or 7.4B (continued)

GENERAL JOURNAL
PAGE _____

	DATE	DESCRIPTION	POST. REF.	DEBIT	CREDIT	
1						1
2						2
3						3
4						4
5						5
6						6
7						7
8						8
9						9
10						10
11						11
12						12
13						13

GENERAL LEDGER

ACCOUNT _____ ACCOUNT NO. _____

DATE	DESCRIPTION	POST. REF.	DEBIT	CREDIT	BALANCE	
					DEBIT	CREDIT

ACCOUNT _____ ACCOUNT NO. _____

DATE	DESCRIPTION	POST. REF.	DEBIT	CREDIT	BALANCE	
					DEBIT	CREDIT

ACCOUNT _____ ACCOUNT NO. _____

DATE	DESCRIPTION	POST. REF.	DEBIT	CREDIT	BALANCE	
					DEBIT	CREDIT

PROBLEM 7.4A or 7.4B (continued)

ACCOUNTS RECEIVABLE SUBSIDIARY LEDGER

NAME _____ TERMS _____

DATE	DESCRIPTION	POST. REF.	DEBIT	CREDIT	BALANCE

NAME _____ TERMS _____

DATE	DESCRIPTION	POST. REF.	DEBIT	CREDIT	BALANCE

NAME _____ TERMS _____

DATE	DESCRIPTION	POST. REF.	DEBIT	CREDIT	BALANCE

NAME _____ TERMS _____

DATE	DESCRIPTION	POST. REF.	DEBIT	CREDIT	BALANCE

NAME _____ TERMS _____

DATE	DESCRIPTION	POST. REF.	DEBIT	CREDIT	BALANCE

PROBLEM 7.4A or 7.4B (continued)

ACCOUNTS RECEIVABLE SUBSIDIARY LEDGER

NAME _____   TERMS _____

	DATE	DESCRIPTION	POST. REF.	DEBIT	CREDIT	BALANCE

Balance of Accounts Receivable account: _____

Analyze: _____

_____

CRITICAL THINKING PROBLEM 7.1

SALES JOURNAL   PAGE _____

	DATE	SALES SLIP NO.	CUSTOMER'S NAME	POST. REF.	ACCOUNTS RECEIVABLE DR./ SALES CR.	
1						1
2						2
3						3
4						4
5						5
6						6
7						7
8						8
9						9
10						10
11						11

CRITICAL THINKING PROBLEM 7.1 (continued)

GENERAL JOURNAL

PAGE _____

	DATE	DESCRIPTION	POST. REF.	DEBIT	CREDIT	
1						1
2						2
3						3
4						4
5						5
6						6
7						7

GENERAL LEDGER

ACCOUNT _____   ACCOUNT NO. _____

DATE	DESCRIPTION	POST. REF.	DEBIT	CREDIT	BALANCE DEBIT	BALANCE CREDIT

ACCOUNT _____   ACCOUNT NO. _____

DATE	DESCRIPTION	POST. REF.	DEBIT	CREDIT	BALANCE DEBIT	BALANCE CREDIT

ACCOUNT _____   ACCOUNT NO. _____

DATE	DESCRIPTION	POST. REF.	DEBIT	CREDIT	BALANCE DEBIT	BALANCE CREDIT

CRITICAL THINKING PROBLEM 7.1 (continued)

ACCOUNTS RECEIVABLE LEDGER

NAME _____ TERMS _____

	DATE	DESCRIPTION	POST. REF.	DEBIT	CREDIT	BALANCE

NAME _____ TERMS _____

	DATE	DESCRIPTION	POST. REF.	DEBIT	CREDIT	BALANCE

NAME _____ TERMS _____

	DATE	DESCRIPTION	POST. REF.	DEBIT	CREDIT	BALANCE

NAME _____ TERMS _____

	DATE	DESCRIPTION	POST. REF.	DEBIT	CREDIT	BALANCE

NAME _____ TERMS _____

	DATE	DESCRIPTION	POST. REF.	DEBIT	CREDIT	BALANCE

CRITICAL THINKING PROBLEM 7.1 (continued)

ACCOUNTS RECEIVABLE SUBSIDIARY LEDGER

NAME _____ TERMS _____

	DATE	DESCRIPTION	POST. REF.	DEBIT	CREDIT	BALANCE

Balance of Accounts Receivable account: _____

Analyze: _____

_____

CRITICAL THINKING PROBLEM 7.2

1. _____

_____

_____

_____

2. _____

_____

_____

_____

_____

3. _____

_____

_____

_____

_____

_____

4. _____

_____

_____

_____

_____

_____

Chapter 7 Practice Test Answer Key

Part A True-False

1. T	11. F
2. T	12. F
3. T	13. T
4. T	14. T
5. T	15. T
6. T	16. T
7. F	17. F
8. F	18. F
9. F	19. F
10. F	20. T

Part B Matching

1. b
2. f
3. d
4. g
5. c
6. a
7. e

Part C Exercises

1. The balance was carried over from December 2015.
2. By referring to a copy of Sales Slip 101.
3. It was most likely a sales return or allowance. Refer to the January 18 entry on page 1 of the general journal.

CHAPTER 8

Accounting for Purchases and Accounts Payable

STUDY GUIDE

Understanding the Chapter

Objectives

1. Record purchases of merchandise on credit in a three-column purchases journal. 2. Post from the three-column purchases journal to the general ledger accounts. 3. Post credit purchases from the purchases journal to the accounts payable subsidiary ledger. 4. Record purchases returns and allowances in the general journal and post them to the accounts payable subsidiary ledger. 5. Prepare a schedule of accounts payable. 6. Compute the net delivered cost of purchases. 7. Demonstrate a knowledge of the procedures for effective internal control of purchases. 8. Record purchases, sales, and returns using the perpetual inventory system. 9. Define the accounting terms new to this chapter.

Reading Assignment

Read Chapter 8 in the textbook. Complete the textbook Section Self Review as you finish reading each section of the chapter, and the Comprehensive Self Review at the end of the chapter. Refer to the Chapter 8 Glossary or to the Glossary at the end of the book to find definitions for terms that are not familiar to you.

Activities

❏ **Thinking Critically**

Answer the *Thinking Critically* questions for Williams-Sonoma and Managerial Implications.

❏ **Discussion Questions**

Answer each assigned discussion question in Chapter 8.

❏ **Exercises**

Complete each assigned exercise in Chapter 8. Use the forms provided in this SGWP. The objectives covered by an exercise are given after the exercise number. If you need help with an exercise, review the portion of the chapter related to the objective(s) covered.

❏ **Problems A/B**

Complete each assigned problem in Chapter 8. Use the forms provided in this SGWP. The objectives covered by a problem are given after the problem number. If you need help with a problem, review the portion of the chapter related to the objective(s) covered.

❏ **Critical Thinking Problems**

Complete the critical thinking problems as assigned. Use the forms provided in this SGWP.

❏ **Business Connections**

Complete the Business Connections activities as assigned to gain a deeper understanding of Chapter 8 concepts.

Practice Tests

Complete the Practice Tests, which cover the main points in your reading assignment. Compare your answers with those in the Practice Test Answer Key for Chapter 8 at the end of this chapter. If you have answered any questions incorrectly, review the related section of the text.

Part A True-False *For each of the following statements, circle T in the answer column if the statement is true or F if the statement is false.*

T   F   **1.** The special purchases journal is used to record all transactions in which merchandise or equipment is purchased on credit.

T   F   **2.** A receiving report is prepared to show the quantity of goods received and their condition.

T   F   **3.** Freight In becomes part of the cost of purchases shown in the Cost of Goods Sold section of the income statement.

T   F   **4.** The procedure for posting totals from the purchases journal remains the same, whether or not an accounts payable ledger is used.

T   F   **5.** Within the accounts payable ledger, the accounts for creditors are arranged alphabetically or by account number.

T   F   **6.** After all postings for a period are completed, the total of the individual balances in the accounts payable ledger should be equal to the balance of the **Accounts Receivable** control account in the general ledger.

T   F   **7.** As soon as it is recorded in the **Purchases** journal, the amount of a purchase is posted as a credit to the supplier's account in the accounts payable ledger.

T   F   **8.** A payment is first recorded in the cash payments journal and then debited immediately to the supplier's account in the accounts payable ledger.

T   F   **9.** The Merchandise Inventory account is debited for purchases of merchandise when the perpetual inventory system is used.

T   F   **10.** At the end of the month, the total of the payments made to creditors is debited to the **Accounts Payable** general ledger account.

T   F   **11.** Payments made to creditors are recorded in the cash payments journal.

T   F   **12.** Purchases Returns and Allowances is a contra-revenue account.

T   F   **13.** Returns of merchandise to suppliers are recorded in the general journal.

T   F   **14.** At the end of the month, the total of the Accounts Payable column in the purchases journal is debited to the **Accounts Payable** control account.

T   F   **15.** The balance of each creditor's account in the accounts payable subsidiary ledger is not computed until the end of the accounting period.

T   F   **16.** One of the basic advantages of the purchases journal is that the posting to **Accounts Payable** is simplified.

T   F   **17.** Each purchase of merchandise on credit should be recorded in the sales journal as it occurs during the month.

T   F   **18.** An account called **Purchases** is charged with the cost of the merchandise as it is sold.

T   F   **19.** The Purchases Returns and Allowances account is credited for merchandise returns when the perpetual inventory system is used.

T   F   **20.** When properly designed, a purchases journal makes posting to the general ledger unnecessary.

Part B Exercise   *Answer each of the following in the space provided. Make your answers complete but as brief as possible.*

A firm uses a multicolumn purchases journal with the following money columns: Accounts Payable Credit, Purchases Debit, and Freight In Debit.

1. How is the **Purchases** account classified?

_____
_____
_____
_____

2. Which columns are totaled and summary posted to the general ledger?

_____
_____
_____
_____

3. How is the accuracy of the totals verified at the end of the month?

_____
_____
_____
_____

4. If the buyer pays freight charges directly to the carrier on a purchase of merchandise, where is the freight transaction recorded?

_____
_____
_____
_____

5. Where is the **Freight In** account shown on the income statement?

_____
_____
_____
_____

6. Where would you record the purchase of office equipment on open account credit terms?

_____
_____
_____
_____

7. The figures of which column are used to update the accounts payable subsidiary ledger?

_____
_____
_____
_____

Demonstration Problem

Santa Rosa Office Supply is a retail business that sells office equipment, furniture, and office supplies. Its credit purchases and purchases returns and allowances for the month of October 2016 follow. The general ledger accounts used to record these transactions are given below.

Instructions

1. Open the general ledger accounts and enter the balance of Accounts Payable for October 1, 2016.

2. Using the list of creditors that follows, open the accounts in the accounts payable subsidiary ledger and enter the account balances for October 1, 2016.

3. Record the transactions in a purchases journal, page 12, and a general journal, page 30.

4. Post individual entries from the purchases journal to the accounts payable subsidiary ledger, then post from the general journal to the general ledger and accounts payable subsidiary ledger.

5. Total, prove, and rule the purchases journal as of October 31, 2016.

6. Post the column totals from the purchases journal to the appropriate general ledger accounts.

7. Compute the net delivered cost of the firm's purchases for the month.

8. Prepare a schedule of accounts payable for October 31, 2016.

9. Check the total of the schedule of accounts payable against the balance of the **Accounts Payable** account in the general ledger. The two amounts should be equal.

GENERAL LEDGER ACCOUNTS

205 Accounts Payable	$18,900 Cr.
501 Purchases	
502 Freight In	
503 Purchases Returns and Allowances	

CREDITORS

Name	Terms	Balance
Bermudez Office Supplies	n/30	
Dallas Office Supply	n/60	$2,320
Davis Office Products	n/30	
Santa Ana Office Center	2/10, n/30	5,670
Thanh Copy and Paper	1/10, n/30	10,910

DATE	TRANSACTIONS
October 4	Purchased desks for $9,160 plus a freight charge of $280 from Davis Office Products, Invoice 3124 dated September 30, terms payable in 30 days.
9	Purchased computers for $7,950 from Bermudez Office Supplies, Invoice 7129 dated October 4, net due and payable in 30 days.
11	Received Credit Memo 165 for $600 from Davis Office Products as an allowance for slightly damaged but usable desks purchased on Invoice 3124 of September 30.
16	Purchased file cabinets for $2,720 plus a freight charge of $124 from Dallas Office Supply, Invoice 9088 dated October 11, terms of 60 days.
21	Purchased electronic calculators for $1,680 from Bermudez Office Supplies, Invoice 7765 dated October 16, net due and payable in 30 days.
24	Purchased laser printer paper for $3,150 plus a freight charge of $320 from Thanh Copy and Paper on Invoice 4891 dated October 19, terms of 1/10, n/30.
29	Received Credit Memo 629 for $540 from Bermudez Office Supplies for defective calculators that were returned. The calculators were originally purchased on Invoice 2765 of October 16.
31	Purchased office chairs for $4,175 plus a freight charge of $156 from Santa Ana Office Center, Invoice 966 dated October 26, terms of 2/10, n/30.

SOLUTION

PURCHASES JOURNAL

DATE		CUSTOMER'S NAME	INVOICE NUMBER	INVOICE DATE	TERMS	POST. REF.	ACCOUNTS PAYABLE CREDIT	PURCHASES DEBIT	FREIGHT IN DEBIT
2016									
Oct.	4	**Davis Office Products**	3124	9/30	n/30		9 4 4 0 00	9 1 6 0 00	2 8 0 00
	9	**Bermudez Office Supplies**	7129	10/4	n/30		7 9 5 0 00	7 9 5 0 00	
	16	**Dallas Office Supply**	9088	10/11	n/60		2 8 4 4 00	2 7 2 0 00	1 2 4 00
	21	**Bermudez Office Supplies**	7765	10/16	n/30		1 6 8 0 00	1 6 8 0 00	
	24	**Thanh Copy & Paper**	4891	10/19	1/10, n/30		3 4 7 0 00	3 1 5 0 00	3 2 0 00
	31	**Santa Ana Office Center**	966	10/26	2/10, n/30		4 3 3 1 00	4 1 7 5 00	1 5 6 00
	31						29 7 1 5 00	28 8 3 5 00	8 8 0 00

GENERAL JOURNAL

	DATE		DESCRIPTION	POST. REF.	DEBIT	CREDIT	
1	**2016**						1
2	Oct.	11	**Accounts Payable/Davis Office Products**	205 ✔	6 0 0 00		2
3			**Purchases Returns and Allowances**	503		6 0 0 00	3
4			**Received Credit Memo 165 for**				4
5			**damaged merchandise; original**				5
6			**purchase was made on Invoice 3124,**				6
7			**September 30, 2016**				7
8							8
9		29	**Accounts Payable/Bermudez Office Supplies**	205 ✔	5 4 0 00		9
10			**Purchases Returns & Allowances**	503		5 4 0 00	10
11			**Received Credit Memo 629 for damaged**				11
12			**merchandise that was returned;**				12
13			**original purchase was made on**				13
14			**Invoice 2765, October 16, 2016**				14
15							15

SOLUTION (continued)

GENERAL LEDGER

ACCOUNT Accounts Payable   **ACCOUNT NO.** 205

DATE		DESCRIPTION	POST. REF.	DEBIT	CREDIT	BALANCE DEBIT	BALANCE CREDIT
2016							
Oct.	1	Balance	✔				18 9 0 0 00
	11		J30	6 0 0 00			18 3 0 0 00
	29		J30	5 4 0 00			17 7 6 0 00
	31		P12		29 7 1 5 00		47 4 7 5 00

ACCOUNT Purchases   **ACCOUNT NO.** 501

DATE		DESCRIPTION	POST. REF.	DEBIT	CREDIT	BALANCE DEBIT	BALANCE CREDIT
2016							
Oct.	31		P12	28 8 3 5 00		28 8 3 5 00	

ACCOUNT Freight In   **ACCOUNT NO.** 502

DATE		DESCRIPTION	POST. REF.	DEBIT	CREDIT	BALANCE DEBIT	BALANCE CREDIT
2016							
Oct.	31		P12	8 8 0 00		8 8 0 00	

ACCOUNT Purchases Returns and Allowances   **ACCOUNT NO.** 503

DATE		DESCRIPTION	POST. REF.	DEBIT	CREDIT	BALANCE DEBIT	BALANCE CREDIT
2016							
Oct.	11		J30		6 0 0 00		6 0 0 00
	29		J30		5 4 0 00		1 1 4 0 00

Purchases	$28,835
Freight In	880
Delivered Cost of Purchases	$29,715
Less Purchases Returns and Allowances	1,140
Net Delivered Cost of Purchases	$28,575

SOLUTION (continued)

STUDY GUIDE

ACCOUNTS PAYABLE SUBSIDIARY LEDGER

NAME **Bermudez Office Supplies**   TERMS __n/30__

DATE		DESCRIPTION	POST. REF.	DEBIT	CREDIT	BALANCE
2016						
Oct.	9	Invoice 7129, 10/4/16	P12		7 9 5 0 00	7 9 5 0 00
	21	Invoice 7765, 10/16/16	P12		1 6 8 0 00	9 6 3 0 00
	29	CM 629	J30	5 4 0 00		9 0 9 0 00

NAME **Dallas Office Supply**   TERMS __n/60__

DATE		DESCRIPTION	POST. REF.	DEBIT	CREDIT	BALANCE
2016						
Oct.	1	Balance	✔			2 3 2 0 00
	16	Invoice 9088, 10/11/16	P12		2 8 4 4 00	5 1 6 4 00

NAME **Davis Office Products**   TERMS __n/30__

DATE		DESCRIPTION	POST. REF.	DEBIT	CREDIT	BALANCE
2016						
Oct.	4	Invoice 3124, 9/30/16	P12		9 4 4 0 00	9 4 4 0 00
	11	CM 165	J30	6 0 0 00		8 8 4 0 00

NAME **Santa Ana Office Center**   TERMS __2/10, n/30__

DATE		DESCRIPTION	POST. REF.	DEBIT	CREDIT	BALANCE
2016						
Oct.	1	Balance	✔			5 6 7 0 00
	31	Invoice 966, 10/26/16	P12		4 3 3 1 00	10 0 0 1 00

NAME **Thanh Copy and Paper**   TERMS __1/10, n/30__

DATE		DESCRIPTION	POST. REF.	DEBIT	CREDIT	BALANCE
2016						
Oct.	1	Balance	✔			10 9 1 0 00
	24	Invoice 4891, 10/19/16	P12		3 4 7 0 00	14 3 8 0 00

SOLUTION (continued)

Santa Rosa Office Supply

Schedule of Accounts Payable

October 31, 2016

Bermudez Office Supplies	9 0 9 0 00
Dallas Office Supply	5 1 6 4 00
Davis Office Products	8 8 4 0 00
Santa Ana Office Center	10 0 0 1 00
Thanh Copy and Paper	14 3 8 0 00
Total	47 4 7 5 00

WORKING PAPERS

Name _____

EXERCISE 8.1

1. _____   4. _____
2. _____   5. _____
3. _____   6. _____

EXERCISE 8.2

	Dr.	Cr.		Dr.	Cr.
1.	_____	_____	4.	_____	_____
2.	_____	_____	5.	_____	_____
3.	_____	_____	6.	_____	_____

EXERCISE 8.3

PURCHASES JOURNAL

PAGE _____

DATE	PURCHASED FROM	INVOICE NUMBER	INVOICE DATE	TERMS	POST. REF.	ACCOUNTS PAYABLE CREDIT	PURCHASES DEBIT	FREIGHT IN DEBIT

EXERCISE 8.4

GENERAL JOURNAL

PAGE _____

	DATE	DESCRIPTION	POST. REF.	DEBIT	CREDIT	
1						1
2						2
3						3
4						4
5						5
6						6
7						7
8						8
9						9
10						10

EXERCISE 8.5

GENERAL JOURNAL　　　　　　　　PAGE _____

	DATE		DESCRIPTION	POST. REF.	DEBIT	CREDIT	
1							1
2							2
3							3
4							4
5							5
6							6
7							7

EXERCISE 8.6

_____
_____
_____
_____
_____
_____
_____

EXERCISE 8.7

a. _____
_____

b. _____
_____

c. _____

d. _____
_____

EXERCISE 8.8

a. _____

b. _____

c. _____

d. _____

EXERCISE 8.9

GENERAL JOURNAL

PAGE _____

DATE		DESCRIPTION	POST. REF.	DEBIT		CREDIT		
								1
								2
								3
								4
								5
								6
								7
								8
								9
								10
								11
								12
								13
								14
								15
								16
								17
								18
								19
								20
								21
								22
								23
								24
								25
								26
								27
								28

PROBLEM 8.1A or 8.1B

PURCHASES JOURNAL   PAGE _____

DATE	PURCHASED FROM	INVOICE NUMBER	INVOICE DATE	TERMS	POST. REF.	ACCOUNTS PAYABLE CREDIT	PURCHASES DEBIT	FREIGHT IN DEBIT

GENERAL JOURNAL   PAGE _____

	DATE	DESCRIPTION	POST. REF.	DEBIT	CREDIT	
1						1
2						2
3						3
4						4
5						5
6						6
7						7
8						8
9						9
10						10
11						11
12						12
13						13
14						14
15						15
16						16
17						17
18						18
19						19

PROBLEM 8.1A or 8.1B (continued)

GENERAL LEDGER

ACCOUNT _____ ACCOUNT NO. _____

DATE	DESCRIPTION	POST. REF.	DEBIT	CREDIT	BALANCE	
					DEBIT	CREDIT

ACCOUNT _____ ACCOUNT NO. _____

DATE	DESCRIPTION	POST. REF.	DEBIT	CREDIT	BALANCE	
					DEBIT	CREDIT

ACCOUNT _____ ACCOUNT NO. _____

DATE	DESCRIPTION	POST. REF.	DEBIT	CREDIT	BALANCE	
					DEBIT	CREDIT

ACCOUNT _____ ACCOUNT NO. _____

DATE	DESCRIPTION	POST. REF.	DEBIT	CREDIT	BALANCE	
					DEBIT	CREDIT

_____

_____

_____

_____

Analyze: _____

PROBLEM 8.2A or 8.2B

ACCOUNTS PAYABLE SUBSIDIARY LEDGER

NAME _____ TERMS _____

DATE	DESCRIPTION	POST. REF.	DEBIT	CREDIT	BALANCE

NAME _____ TERMS _____

DATE	DESCRIPTION	POST. REF.	DEBIT	CREDIT	BALANCE

NAME _____ TERMS _____

DATE	DESCRIPTION	POST. REF.	DEBIT	CREDIT	BALANCE

NAME _____ TERMS _____

DATE	DESCRIPTION	POST. REF.	DEBIT	CREDIT	BALANCE

NAME _____ TERMS _____

DATE	DESCRIPTION	POST. REF.	DEBIT	CREDIT	BALANCE

PROBLEM 8.2A or 8.2B (continued)

Analyze: _____

EXTRA FORM

PROBLEM 8.3A or 8.3B

PURCHASES JOURNAL

PAGE _____

DATE		PURCHASED FROM	INVOICE NUMBER	INVOICE DATE	TERMS	POST. REF.	ACCOUNTS PAYABLE CREDIT	PURCHASES DEBIT	FREIGHT IN DEBIT

GENERAL JOURNAL

PAGE _____

	DATE		DESCRIPTION	POST. REF.	DEBIT	CREDIT	
1							1
2							2
3							3
4							4
5							5
6							6
7							7
8							8
9							9
10							10
11							11
12							12
13							13
14							14
15							15

PROBLEM 8.3A or 8.3B (continued)

GENERAL LEDGER

ACCOUNT _____   ACCOUNT NO. _____

DATE	DESCRIPTION	POST. REF.	DEBIT	CREDIT	BALANCE	
					DEBIT	CREDIT

ACCOUNT _____   ACCOUNT NO. _____

DATE	DESCRIPTION	POST. REF.	DEBIT	CREDIT	BALANCE	
					DEBIT	CREDIT

ACCOUNT _____   ACCOUNT NO. _____

DATE	DESCRIPTION	POST. REF.	DEBIT	CREDIT	BALANCE	
					DEBIT	CREDIT

ACCOUNT _____   ACCOUNT NO. _____

DATE	DESCRIPTION	POST. REF.	DEBIT	CREDIT	BALANCE	
					DEBIT	CREDIT

_____

_____

_____

_____

_____

PROBLEM 8.3A or 8.3B (continued)

ACCOUNTS PAYABLE SUBSIDIARY LEDGER

NAME _____ TERMS _____

DATE		DESCRIPTION	POST. REF.	DEBIT	CREDIT	BALANCE

NAME _____ TERMS _____

DATE		DESCRIPTION	POST. REF.	DEBIT	CREDIT	BALANCE

NAME _____ TERMS _____

DATE		DESCRIPTION	POST. REF.	DEBIT	CREDIT	BALANCE

NAME _____ TERMS _____

DATE		DESCRIPTION	POST. REF.	DEBIT	CREDIT	BALANCE

NAME _____ TERMS _____

DATE		DESCRIPTION	POST. REF.	DEBIT	CREDIT	BALANCE

PROBLEM 8.3A or 8.3B (continued)

Analyze: _____

EXTRA FORMS

NAME _____ TERMS _____

DATE	DESCRIPTION	POST. REF.	DEBIT	CREDIT	BALANCE

NAME _____ TERMS _____

DATE	DESCRIPTION	POST. REF.	DEBIT	CREDIT	BALANCE

PROBLEM 8.4A or 8.4B

PURCHASES JOURNAL   PAGE _____

DATE	PURCHASED FROM	INVOICE NUMBER	INVOICE DATE	TERMS	POST. REF.	ACCOUNTS PAYABLE CREDIT	PURCHASES DEBIT	FREIGHT IN DEBIT

GENERAL JOURNAL   PAGE _____

	DATE	DESCRIPTION	POST. REF.	DEBIT	CREDIT	
1						1
2						2
3						3
4						4
5						5
6						6
7						7
8						8
9						9
10						10
11						11
12						12
13						13
14						14
15						15

Name _____

PROBLEM 8.4A or 8.4B (continued)

GENERAL LEDGER

ACCOUNT _____ ACCOUNT NO. _____

DATE	DESCRIPTION	POST. REF.	DEBIT	CREDIT	BALANCE	
					DEBIT	CREDIT

ACCOUNT _____ ACCOUNT NO. _____

DATE	DESCRIPTION	POST. REF.	DEBIT	CREDIT	BALANCE	
					DEBIT	CREDIT

ACCOUNT _____ ACCOUNT NO. _____

DATE	DESCRIPTION	POST. REF.	DEBIT	CREDIT	BALANCE	
					DEBIT	CREDIT

ACCOUNT _____ ACCOUNT NO. _____

DATE	DESCRIPTION	POST. REF.	DEBIT	CREDIT	BALANCE	
					DEBIT	CREDIT

Net Delivered Cost of Purchases

_____

_____

_____

_____

_____

PROBLEM 8.4A or 8.4B (continued)

ACCOUNTS PAYABLE SUBSIDIARY LEDGER

NAME _____ TERMS _____

	DATE	DESCRIPTION	POST. REF.	DEBIT	CREDIT	BALANCE

NAME _____ TERMS _____

	DATE	DESCRIPTION	POST. REF.	DEBIT	CREDIT	BALANCE

NAME _____ TERMS _____

	DATE	DESCRIPTION	POST. REF.	DEBIT	CREDIT	BALANCE

NAME _____ TERMS _____

	DATE	DESCRIPTION	POST. REF.	DEBIT	CREDIT	BALANCE

NAME _____ TERMS _____

	DATE	DESCRIPTION	POST. REF.	DEBIT	CREDIT	BALANCE

PROBLEM 8.4A or 8.4B (continued)

Analyze:

EXTRA FORM

CRITICAL THINKING PROBLEM 8.1

PURCHASES JOURNAL

PAGE _____

DATE	PURCHASED FROM	INVOICE NUMBER	INVOICE DATE	TERMS	POST. REF.	ACCOUNTS PAYABLE CREDIT	PURCHASES DEBIT	FREIGHT IN DEBIT

SALES JOURNAL

PAGE _____

	DATE	SALES SLIP NO.	CUSTOMER'S NAME	POST. REF.	ACCOUNTS RECEIVABLE DEBIT	SALES TAX PAYABLE CREDIT	SALES CREDIT	
1								1
2								2
3								3
4								4
5								5
6								6
7								7
8								8
9								9
10								10
11								11
12								12
13								13
14								14
15								15

CRITICAL THINKING PROBLEM 8.1 (continued)

ACCOUNTS PAYABLE SUBSIDIARY LEDGER

NAME _____ TERMS _____

DATE	DESCRIPTION	POST. REF.	DEBIT	CREDIT	BALANCE

NAME _____ TERMS _____

DATE	DESCRIPTION	POST. REF.	DEBIT	CREDIT	BALANCE

NAME _____ TERMS _____

DATE	DESCRIPTION	POST. REF.	DEBIT	CREDIT	BALANCE

NAME _____ TERMS _____

DATE	DESCRIPTION	POST. REF.	DEBIT	CREDIT	BALANCE

NAME _____ TERMS _____

DATE	DESCRIPTION	POST. REF.	DEBIT	CREDIT	BALANCE

NAME _____ TERMS _____

DATE	DESCRIPTION	POST. REF.	DEBIT	CREDIT	BALANCE

CRITICAL THINKING PROBLEM 8.1 (continued)

ACCOUNTS PAYABLE SUBSIDIARY LEDGER

NAME _____ TERMS _____

	DATE	DESCRIPTION	POST. REF.	DEBIT	CREDIT	BALANCE

NAME _____ TERMS _____

	DATE	DESCRIPTION	POST. REF.	DEBIT	CREDIT	BALANCE

ACCOUNTS RECEIVABLE SUBSIDIARY LEDGER

NAME _____ TERMS _____

	DATE	DESCRIPTION	POST. REF.	DEBIT	CREDIT	BALANCE

NAME _____ TERMS _____

	DATE	DESCRIPTION	POST. REF.	DEBIT	CREDIT	BALANCE

NAME _____ TERMS _____

	DATE	DESCRIPTION	POST. REF.	DEBIT	CREDIT	BALANCE

CRITICAL THINKING PROBLEM 8.1 (continued)

ACCOUNTS RECEIVABLE SUBSIDIARY LEDGER

NAME _____ TERMS _____

	DATE	DESCRIPTION	POST. REF.	DEBIT	CREDIT	BALANCE

NAME _____ TERMS _____

	DATE	DESCRIPTION	POST. REF.	DEBIT	CREDIT	BALANCE

NAME _____ TERMS _____

	DATE	DESCRIPTION	POST. REF.	DEBIT	CREDIT	BALANCE

NAME _____ TERMS _____

	DATE	DESCRIPTION	POST. REF.	DEBIT	CREDIT	BALANCE

NAME _____ TERMS _____

	DATE	DESCRIPTION	POST. REF.	DEBIT	CREDIT	BALANCE

NAME _____ TERMS _____

	DATE	DESCRIPTION	POST. REF.	DEBIT	CREDIT	BALANCE

CRITICAL THINKING PROBLEM 8.1 (continued)

ACCOUNTS RECEIVABLE SUBSIDIARY LEDGER

NAME _____ TERMS _____

DATE	DESCRIPTION	POST. REF.	DEBIT	CREDIT	BALANCE

NAME _____ TERMS _____

DATE	DESCRIPTION	POST. REF.	DEBIT	CREDIT	BALANCE

GENERAL LEDGER

ACCOUNT _____ ACCOUNT NO. _____

DATE	DESCRIPTION	POST. REF.	DEBIT	CREDIT	BALANCE DEBIT	BALANCE CREDIT

ACCOUNT _____ ACCOUNT NO. _____

DATE	DESCRIPTION	POST. REF.	DEBIT	CREDIT	BALANCE DEBIT	BALANCE CREDIT

ACCOUNT _____ ACCOUNT NO. _____

DATE	DESCRIPTION	POST. REF.	DEBIT	CREDIT	BALANCE DEBIT	BALANCE CREDIT

ACCOUNT _____ ACCOUNT NO. _____

DATE	DESCRIPTION	POST. REF.	DEBIT	CREDIT	BALANCE DEBIT	BALANCE CREDIT

CRITICAL THINKING PROBLEM 8.1 (continued)

GENERAL LEDGER

ACCOUNT _____ ACCOUNT NO. _____

DATE	DESCRIPTION	POST. REF.	DEBIT	CREDIT	BALANCE DEBIT	BALANCE CREDIT

ACCOUNT _____ ACCOUNT NO. _____

DATE	DESCRIPTION	POST. REF.	DEBIT	CREDIT	BALANCE DEBIT	BALANCE CREDIT

CRITICAL THINKING PROBLEM 8.1 (continued)

Analyze: _____

CRITICAL THINKING PROBLEM 8.2

_____
_____
_____
_____
_____
_____
_____
_____
_____
_____
_____
_____
_____
_____
_____
_____
_____
_____
_____
_____
_____
_____

Chapter 8 Practice Test Answer Key

Part A True-False

1.	F	11.	T
2.	T	12.	F
3.	T	13.	T
4.	T	14.	F
5.	T	15.	F
6.	F	16.	T
7.	T	17.	F
8.	T	18.	F
9.	T	19.	F
10.	T	20.	F

Part B Exercises

1. An Expense.
2. All Columns.
3. Accounts Payable Credit = Purchases Debit + Freight In Debit.
4. It is not recorded in the purchases journal at all; it is entered in the cash payments journal.
5. In the Cost of Goods Sold Section.
6. The General Journal.
7. The Accounts Payable Column.

CHAPTER 9

Cash Receipts, Cash Payments, and Banking Procedures

STUDY GUIDE

Understanding the Chapter

Objectives

1. Record cash receipts in a cash receipts journal. **2.** Account for cash short or over. **3.** Post from the cash receipts journal to subsidiary and general ledgers. **4.** Record cash payments in a cash payments journal. **5.** Post from the cash payments journal to subsidiary and general ledgers. **6.** Demonstrate a knowledge of procedures for a petty cash fund. **7.** Demonstrate a knowledge of internal control routines for cash. **8.** Write a check, endorse checks, prepare a bank deposit slip, and maintain a checkbook balance. **9.** Reconcile the monthly bank statement. **10.** Record any adjusting entries required from the bank reconciliation. **11.** Understand how businesses use online banking to manage cash activities. **12.** Record cash payments and cash receipts using the perpetual inventory system. **13.** Define accounting terms new to this chapter.

Reading Assignment

Read Chapter 9 in the textbook. Complete the Section Self Review as you finish reading each section of the chapter, and the Comprehensive Self Review at the end of the chapter. Refer to the Chapter 9 Glossary or to the Glossary at the end of the book to find definitions for terms that are not familiar to you.

Activities

❏ **Thinking Critically**

Answer the *Thinking Critically* questions for CLIF Bars and Managerial Implications

❏ **Discussion Questions**

Answer each assigned review question in Chapter 9.

❏ **Exercises**

Complete each assigned exercise in Chapter 9. Use the forms provided in this SGWP. The objectives covered by an exercise are given after the exercise number. If you need help with an exercise, review the portion of the chapter related to the objective(s) covered.

❏ **Problems A/B**

Complete each assigned problem in Chapter 9. Use the forms provided in this SGWP. The objectives covered by a problem are given after the problem number. If you need help with a problem, review the portion of the chapter related to the objective(s) covered.

❏ **Critical Thinking Problems**

Complete the critical thinking problems as assigned. Use the forms provided in this SGWP.

❏ **Business Connections**

Complete the Business Connections activities as assigned to gain a deeper understanding of Chapter 9 concepts.

Practice Tests

Complete the Practice Tests, which cover the main points in your reading assignment. Compare your answers with those in the Practice Test Answer Key for Chapter 9 at the end of this chapter. If you have answered any questions incorrectly, review the related section of the text.

Part A True-False *For each of the following statements, circle T in the answer column if the statement is true or F if the statement is false.*

T   F   **1.** Account numbers are recorded below the totals of each column as each summary posting from the cash payments journal is completed.

T   F   **2.** The title of a special journal makes it possible to omit much of the explanation that would be needed in a general journal entry.

T   F   **3.** A cash investment by the owner in a business should be recorded in the cash receipts journal.

T   F   **4.** The **Sales Tax Payable** account represents a liability of the business.

T   F   **5.** Cash received by mail should be deposited by the same person who accepts and lists it.

T   F   **6.** **Cash Short or Over** is a general ledger account that normally has a credit balance because cash tends to be short more often than over.

T   F   **7.** Only checks are listed on the deposit slip.

T   F   **8.** Checks can be identified on a deposit slip by the use of the American Bankers Association transit numbers.

T   F   **9.** Checks made payable to cash or to bearer need not be endorsed when deposited.

T   F   **10.** The money represented by deposited checks becomes available for use as soon as the deposit is made.

T   F   **11.** The best form of endorsement for business purposes is the restrictive endorsement, which limits the use of the check to a stated purpose.

T   F   **12.** Internal controls are not necessary if payments are made by check.

T   F   **13.** Except for petty cash payments, all payments should be made by check.

T   F   **14.** Correct internal control procedures require that the approval for paying all bills, writing all checks, and signing all checks should be the responsibility of the same person.

T   F   **15.** An adequate system of internal control over cash will provide for safeguarding both incoming and outgoing funds.

T   F   **16.** Each petty cash payment is entered separately in the cash payments journal.

T   F   **17.** The petty cash analysis sheet is a memorandum record of petty cash payments rather than a record of original entry.

T   F   **18.** When posting from the cash payments journal at the end of the month, the accountant posts the total cash payments as a single credit to cash.

T   F   **19.** The check to replenish the petty cash fund is written for an amount sufficient to restore the fund to its established balance.

T   F   **20.** The abbreviation "CP5" in the Posting Reference column of a ledger account indicates that the posting was made from the cash receipts journal on the fifth day of the month.

T   F   **21.** The Other Accounts Debit column of a cash payments journal is used to record the debits that are to be posted individually.

T F **22.** Once created, login information for online bank account access should not be changed.

T F **23.** The Purchases Discounts account is credited for cash discounts taken by the purchaser when the perpetual inventory system is used.

Part B Matching

For each numbered item, choose the matching term from the box and write the identifying letter in the answer column.

_____ **1.** The firm or person designated on the check to receive payment.

_____ **2.** The person or firm from whose account a check is to be paid.

_____ **3.** The form that contains all the information necessary for journalizing a transaction paid by check.

_____ **4.** A check on which payment has been refused because of too few funds in the issuer's account.

_____ **5.** The process of determining why a difference exists between the firm's accounting records and the bank records and bringing them into balance.

_____ **6.** Receipts that have been deposited and entered in the firm's accounting records but have not yet been entered on the bank's records.

_____ **7.** Checks issued and recorded that have not been paid by the bank.

_____ **8.** A form received from the bank showing all transactions recorded in the depositor's account during the month.

_____ **9.** A form on which all cash and cash items are listed before they are placed in the bank.

_____ **10.** A written promise to pay a specific amount at a specific time.

_____ **11.** The process by which a single amount is posted instead of each entry being posted separately.

_____ **12.** A system designed to safeguard assets and to help ensure the accuracy and reliability of accounting records.

_____ **13.** An electronic transfer of money from one account to another.

a. NSF Check
b. Deposit in Transit
c. Outstanding checks
d. Bank reconciliation
e. Bank statement
f. Stub
g. Payee
h. Drawer
i. Deposit slip
j. Promissory note
k. Summary posting
l. Internal control
m. EFT

Demonstration Problem

On June 2, 2016, Rancho Santiago Legal Services received its May bank statement. Enclosed with the bank statement, shown below, was a debit memorandum for $150 for a NSF check issued by James Greene. Additionally, Check No. 177 was correctly drawn for $400 in payment of a utility bill, but was mistakenly recorded by Rancho Santiago Legal Services as $40. The firm's checkbook contained the information shown below about deposits made and checks issued during May. The balance of the **Cash** account and the checkbook on May 31 was $37,425.

Instructions

1. Prepare a bank reconciliation statement for Rancho Santiago Legal Services as of May 31, 2016.

2. Record general journal entries for any items on the bank reconciliation statement that must be journalized. Date the entries May 31, 2016. Number the journal as page 17.

Checkbook information:

May 1	Balance	$40,592
1	Check 177	40
1	Check 178	800
7	Deposit	2,600
8	Check 179	900
12	Check 180	6,000
17	Check 181	720
19	Deposit	680
22	Check 182	88
23	Check 183	592
26	Deposit	1,848
29	Check 184	160
31	Deposit	925
		$37,345

First California National Bank

Rancho Santiago Legal Services
4312 Brea Street
Yorba Linda, CA 92885-8714

ACCOUNT NO. 77546798
PERIOD ENDING: May 31, 2016

CHECK NO.	AMOUNT	DATE	DESCRIPTION	BALANCE
			Balance last statement	40,592.00
177	400.00	6/1		40,192.00
178	800.00	6/4		39,392.00
	2,600.00	6/7	Deposit	41,992.00
179	900.00	6/8		41,092.00
180	6,000.00	6/12		35,092.00
	150.00	6/12	Debit Memorandum	34,942.00
181	720.00	6/17		34,222.00
	680.00	6/19	Deposit	34,902.00
182	88.00	6/22		34,814.00
	1,848.00	6/26	Deposit	36,662.00
	25.00	6/29	Service Charge	36,637.00

SOLUTION

Rancho Santiago Legal Services

Bank Reconciliation Statement

May 31, 2016

Balance on Bank Statement			36 6 3 7 00
Additions:			
Deposit of May 31 in Transit			9 2 5 00
			37 5 6 2 00
Deductions for Outstanding Checks:			
Check 183 of May 23	5 9 2 00		
Check 184 of May 29	1 6 0 00		
Total Checks Outstanding			7 5 2 00
Adjusted Bank Balance			36 8 1 0 00
Balance in Books			37 3 4 5 00
Deductions:			
NSF Check	1 5 0 00		
Recording Error, Check 177	3 6 0 00		
Bank Service Charge	2 5 00		5 3 5 00
Adjusted Book Balance			36 8 1 0 00

GENERAL JOURNAL

PAGE ___17___

	DATE		DESCRIPTION	POST. REF.	DEBIT	CREDIT	
1	2016						1
2	May	31	Accounts Receivable/James Greene		1 5 0 00		2
3			Cash			1 5 0 00	3
4			To record NSF check returned by bank				4
5							5
6		31	Miscellaneous Expense		2 5 00		6
7			Cash			2 5 00	7
8			To record bank service charge for May				8
9							9
10		31	Utilities Expense		3 6 0 00		10
11			Cash			3 6 0 00	11
12			To correct error for check 177 of May 1				12
13							13

WORKING PAPERS

Name _____

EXERCISES 9.1, 9.2

EXERCISE 9.1

CASH RECEIPTS JOURNAL

PAGE ____

DATE	DESCRIPTION	POST. REF.	ACCOUNTS RECEIVABLE CREDIT	SALES TAX PAYABLE CREDIT	SALES CREDIT	OTHER ACCOUNTS CREDIT			CASH DEBIT
						ACCOUNT NAME	POST. REF.	AMOUNT	

EXERCISE 9.2

CASH PAYMENTS JOURNAL

PAGE ____

DATE	CK. NO.	DESCRIPTION	POST. REF.	ACCOUNTS PAYABLE DEBIT	OTHER ACCOUNTS DEBIT			PURCHASES DISCOUNT CREDIT	CASH CREDIT
					ACCOUNT NAME	POST. REF.	AMOUNT		

EXERCISES 9.3, 9.4

EXERCISE 9.3

CASH PAYMENTS JOURNAL

PAGE _____

DATE	CK. NO.	DESCRIPTION	POST. REF.	ACCOUNTS PAYABLE DEBIT	OTHER ACCOUNTS DEBIT			PURCHASES DISCOUNT CREDIT	CASH CREDIT
					ACCOUNT NAME	POST. REF.	AMOUNT		

EXERCISE 9.4

CASH PAYMENTS JOURNAL

PAGE _____

DATE	CK. NO.	DESCRIPTION	POST. REF.	ACCOUNTS PAYABLE DEBIT	OTHER ACCOUNTS DEBIT			PURCHASES DISCOUNT CREDIT	CASH CREDIT
					ACCOUNT NAME	POST. REF.	AMOUNT		

EXERCISE 9.5

_____

_____

GENERAL JOURNAL   PAGE _____

	DATE	DESCRIPTION	POST. REF.	DEBIT	CREDIT	
1						1
2						2
3						3
4						4
5						5
6						6
7						7
8						8
9						9
10						10
11						11
12						12
13						13
14						14

EXERCISE 9.6

	Bank Balance	Book Balance	Accounting Entry
1.	_____	_____	_____
2.	_____	_____	_____
3.	_____	_____	_____
4.	_____	_____	_____
5.	_____	_____	_____
6.	_____	_____	_____
7.	_____	_____	_____

EXTRA FORM

_____

_____

GENERAL JOURNAL   PAGE _____

	DATE	DESCRIPTION	POST. REF.	DEBIT	CREDIT	
1						1
2						2
3						3
4						4
5						5
6						6
7						7
8						8
9						9
10						10
11						11
12						12
13						13
14						14

EXERCISE 9.7

EXERCISE 9.7 (continued)

GENERAL JOURNAL

PAGE _____

	DATE		DESCRIPTION	POST. REF.	DEBIT	CREDIT	
1							1
2							2
3							3
4							4
5							5
6							6
7							7
8							8
9							9
10							10
11							11
12							12

EXERCISE 9.8

EXERCISE 9.9

_____

_____

GENERAL JOURNAL PAGE 21

	DATE		DESCRIPTION	POST. REF.	DEBIT	CREDIT	
1							1
2							2
3							3
4							4
5							5
6							6
7							7
8							8
9							9
10							10
11							11
12							12
13							13
14							14

EXERCISE 9.10

1.

2.

GENERAL JOURNAL PAGE 10

DATE		DESCRIPTION	POST. REF.	DEBIT	CREDIT	
						1
						2
						3
						4
						5
						6
						7
						8
						9

PROBLEM 9.1A or 9.1B

PAGE ___

CASH RECEIPTS JOURNAL

DATE	DESCRIPTION	POST. REF.	ACCOUNTS RECEIVABLE CREDIT	SALES TAX PAYABLE CREDIT	SALES CREDIT	OTHER ACCOUNTS CREDIT			CASH DEBIT
						ACCOUNT NAME	POST. REF.	AMOUNT	

PROBLEM 9.1A or 9.1B (continued)

GENERAL LEDGER

ACCOUNT _____ ACCOUNT NO. _____

DATE	DESCRIPTION	POST. REF.	DEBIT	CREDIT	BALANCE	
					DEBIT	CREDIT

ACCOUNT _____ ACCOUNT NO. _____

DATE	DESCRIPTION	POST. REF.	DEBIT	CREDIT	BALANCE	
					DEBIT	CREDIT

ACCOUNT _____ ACCOUNT NO. _____

DATE	DESCRIPTION	POST. REF.	DEBIT	CREDIT	BALANCE	
					DEBIT	CREDIT

ACCOUNT _____ ACCOUNT NO. _____

DATE	DESCRIPTION	POST. REF.	DEBIT	CREDIT	BALANCE	
					DEBIT	CREDIT

ACCOUNT _____ ACCOUNT NO. _____

DATE	DESCRIPTION	POST. REF.	DEBIT	CREDIT	BALANCE	
					DEBIT	CREDIT

PROBLEM 9.1A or 9.1B (continued)

GENERAL LEDGER

ACCOUNT _____ ACCOUNT NO. _____

DATE	DESCRIPTION	POST. REF.	DEBIT	CREDIT	BALANCE	
					DEBIT	CREDIT

ACCOUNT _____ ACCOUNT NO. _____

DATE	DESCRIPTION	POST. REF.	DEBIT	CREDIT	BALANCE	
					DEBIT	CREDIT

ACCOUNT _____ ACCOUNT NO. _____

DATE	DESCRIPTION	POST. REF.	DEBIT	CREDIT	BALANCE	
					DEBIT	CREDIT

ACCOUNT _____ ACCOUNT NO. _____

DATE	DESCRIPTION	POST. REF.	DEBIT	CREDIT	BALANCE	
					DEBIT	CREDIT

Analyze: _____

_____

PROBLEM 9.2A or 9.2B

PAGE

CASH PAYMENTS JOURNAL

DATE	CK. NO.	DESCRIPTION	POST. REF.	ACCOUNTS PAYABLE DEBIT	OTHER ACCOUNTS DEBIT			PURCHASES DISCOUNT CREDIT	CASH CREDIT
					ACCOUNT NAME	POST. REF.	AMOUNT		

PROBLEM 9.2A or 9.2B (continued)

PETTY CASH ANALYSIS SHEET

| DATE | VOU. NO. | DESCRIPTION | RECEIPTS | PAYMENTS | DISTRIBUTION OF PAYMENTS |||| OTHER ACCOUNTS DEBIT ||
					SUPPLIES DEBIT	DELIVERY EXPENSE DEBIT	MISC. EXPENSE DEBIT		ACCOUNT NAME	AMOUNT

PROBLEM 9.2A or 9.2B (continued)

GENERAL LEDGER

ACCOUNT _____ ACCOUNT NO. _____

DATE		DESCRIPTION	POST. REF.	DEBIT	CREDIT	BALANCE	
						DEBIT	CREDIT

ACCOUNT _____ ACCOUNT NO. _____

DATE		DESCRIPTION	POST. REF.	DEBIT	CREDIT	BALANCE	
						DEBIT	CREDIT

ACCOUNT _____ ACCOUNT NO. _____

DATE		DESCRIPTION	POST. REF.	DEBIT	CREDIT	BALANCE	
						DEBIT	CREDIT

ACCOUNT _____ ACCOUNT NO. _____

DATE		DESCRIPTION	POST. REF.	DEBIT	CREDIT	BALANCE	
						DEBIT	CREDIT

ACCOUNT _____ ACCOUNT NO. _____

DATE		DESCRIPTION	POST. REF.	DEBIT	CREDIT	BALANCE	
						DEBIT	CREDIT

PROBLEM 9.2A or 9.2B (continued)

GENERAL LEDGER

ACCOUNT _____ ACCOUNT NO. _____

DATE	DESCRIPTION	POST. REF.	DEBIT	CREDIT	BALANCE	
					DEBIT	CREDIT

ACCOUNT _____ ACCOUNT NO. _____

DATE	DESCRIPTION	POST. REF.	DEBIT	CREDIT	BALANCE	
					DEBIT	CREDIT

ACCOUNT _____ ACCOUNT NO. _____

DATE	DESCRIPTION	POST. REF.	DEBIT	CREDIT	BALANCE	
					DEBIT	CREDIT

ACCOUNT _____ ACCOUNT NO. _____

DATE	DESCRIPTION	POST. REF.	DEBIT	CREDIT	BALANCE	
					DEBIT	CREDIT

ACCOUNT _____ ACCOUNT NO. _____

DATE	DESCRIPTION	POST. REF.	DEBIT	CREDIT	BALANCE	
					DEBIT	CREDIT

PROBLEM 9.2A or 9.2B (continued)

GENERAL LEDGER

ACCOUNT _____ ACCOUNT NO. _____

	DATE	DESCRIPTION	POST. REF.	DEBIT	CREDIT	BALANCE	
						DEBIT	CREDIT

ACCOUNT _____ ACCOUNT NO. _____

	DATE	DESCRIPTION	POST. REF.	DEBIT	CREDIT	BALANCE	
						DEBIT	CREDIT

ACCOUNT _____ ACCOUNT NO. _____

	DATE	DESCRIPTION	POST. REF.	DEBIT	CREDIT	BALANCE	
						DEBIT	CREDIT

ACCOUNT _____ ACCOUNT NO. _____

	DATE	DESCRIPTION	POST. REF.	DEBIT	CREDIT	BALANCE	
						DEBIT	CREDIT

ACCOUNT _____ ACCOUNT NO. _____

	DATE	DESCRIPTION	POST. REF.	DEBIT	CREDIT	BALANCE	
						DEBIT	CREDIT

Analyze: _____
_____

PROBLEM 9.3A or 9.3B

SALES JOURNAL

PAGE _____

DATE	INVOICE NO.	CUSTOMER'S NAME	POST. REF.	ACCOUNTS RECEIVABLE DR./ SALES CR.	
					1
					2
					3
					4
					5
					6
					7
					8
					9
					10
					11

CASH RECEIPTS JOURNAL

PAGE _____

DATE	DESCRIPTION	POST. REF.	ACCOUNTS RECEIVABLE CREDIT	SALES CREDIT	OTHER ACCOUNTS CREDIT			SALES DISCOUNTS DEBIT	CASH DEBIT
					ACCOUNT NAME	POST. REF.	AMOUNT		

PROBLEM 9.3A or 9.3B (continued)

GENERAL JOURNAL

PAGE _____

	DATE	DESCRIPTION	POST. REF.	DEBIT	CREDIT	
1						1
2						2
3						3
4						4
5						5
6						6
7						7
8						8
9						9
10						10
11						11
12						12

GENERAL LEDGER (PARTIAL)

ACCOUNT _____ ACCOUNT NO. _____

DATE	DESCRIPTION	POST. REF.	DEBIT	CREDIT	BALANCE	
					DEBIT	CREDIT

ACCOUNT _____ ACCOUNT NO. _____

DATE	DESCRIPTION	POST. REF.	DEBIT	CREDIT	BALANCE	
					DEBIT	CREDIT

ACCOUNT _____ ACCOUNT NO. _____

DATE	DESCRIPTION	POST. REF.	DEBIT	CREDIT	BALANCE	
					DEBIT	CREDIT

PROBLEM 9.3A or 9.3B (continued)

GENERAL LEDGER (PARTIAL)

ACCOUNT _____ ACCOUNT NO. _____

	DATE	DESCRIPTION	POST. REF.	DEBIT	CREDIT	BALANCE	
						DEBIT	CREDIT

ACCOUNT _____ ACCOUNT NO. _____

	DATE	DESCRIPTION	POST. REF.	DEBIT	CREDIT	BALANCE	
						DEBIT	CREDIT

ACCOUNT _____ ACCOUNT NO. _____

	DATE	DESCRIPTION	POST. REF.	DEBIT	CREDIT	BALANCE	
						DEBIT	CREDIT

Analyze: _____

PROBLEM 9.4A or 9.4B

PURCHASES JOURNAL

PAGE _____

DATE		PURCHASED FROM	INVOICE NUMBER	INVOICE DATE	TERMS	POST. REF.	PURCHASES DR./ ACCOUNTS PAYABLE CR.

GENERAL JOURNAL

PAGE _____

	DATE		DESCRIPTION	POST. REF.	DEBIT	CREDIT	
1							1
2							2
3							3
4							4
5							5
6							6
7							7
8							8
9							9
10							10
11							11
12							12
13							13
14							14
15							15
16							16
17							17
18							18
19							19
20							20
21							21
22							22
23							23

PROBLEM 9.4A or 9.4B (continued)

CASH PAYMENTS JOURNAL

PAGE ____

DATE	CK. NO.	DESCRIPTION	POST. REF.	ACCOUNTS PAYABLE DEBIT	OTHER ACCOUNTS DEBIT			PURCHASES DISCOUNT CREDIT	CASH CREDIT
					ACCOUNT NAME	POST. REF.	AMOUNT		

PROBLEM 9.4A or 9.4B (continued)

GENERAL LEDGER

ACCOUNT _____ ACCOUNT NO. _____

DATE	DESCRIPTION	POST. REF.	DEBIT	CREDIT	BALANCE	
					DEBIT	CREDIT

ACCOUNT _____ ACCOUNT NO. _____

DATE	DESCRIPTION	POST. REF.	DEBIT	CREDIT	BALANCE	
					DEBIT	CREDIT

ACCOUNT _____ ACCOUNT NO. _____

DATE	DESCRIPTION	POST. REF.	DEBIT	CREDIT	BALANCE	
					DEBIT	CREDIT

ACCOUNT _____ ACCOUNT NO. _____

DATE	DESCRIPTION	POST. REF.	DEBIT	CREDIT	BALANCE	
					DEBIT	CREDIT

PROBLEM 9.4A or 9.4B (continued)

GENERAL LEDGER

ACCOUNT _____ ACCOUNT NO. _____

DATE	DESCRIPTION	POST. REF.	DEBIT	CREDIT	BALANCE	
					DEBIT	CREDIT

ACCOUNT _____ ACCOUNT NO. _____

DATE	DESCRIPTION	POST. REF.	DEBIT	CREDIT	BALANCE	
					DEBIT	CREDIT

ACCOUNT _____ ACCOUNT NO. _____

DATE	DESCRIPTION	POST. REF.	DEBIT	CREDIT	BALANCE	
					DEBIT	CREDIT

ACCOUNT _____ ACCOUNT NO. _____

DATE	DESCRIPTION	POST. REF.	DEBIT	CREDIT	BALANCE	
					DEBIT	CREDIT

ACCOUNT _____ ACCOUNT NO. _____

DATE	DESCRIPTION	POST. REF.	DEBIT	CREDIT	BALANCE	
					DEBIT	CREDIT

ACCOUNT _____ ACCOUNT NO. _____

DATE	DESCRIPTION	POST. REF.	DEBIT	CREDIT	BALANCE	
					DEBIT	CREDIT

PROBLEM 9.4A or 9.4B (continued)

Analyze:

EXTRA FORM

PROBLEM 9.5A or 9.5B

_____

_____

GENERAL JOURNAL   PAGE _____

	DATE	DESCRIPTION	POST. REF.	DEBIT	CREDIT	
1						1
2						2
3						3
4						4
5						5
6						6
7						7
8						8
9						9
10						10
11						11
12						12
13						13

Analyze: _____

PROBLEM 9.6A or 9.6B

PROBLEM 9.6A or 9.6B (continued)

GENERAL JOURNAL   PAGE _____

	DATE		DESCRIPTION	POST. REF.	DEBIT	CREDIT	
1							1
2							2
3							3
4							4
5							5
6							6
7							7
8							8
9							9
10							10
11							11
12							12
13							13
14							14
15							15
16							16
17							17
18							18
19							19
20							20
21							21
22							22
23							23
24							24
25							25
26							26
27							27
28							28

Analyze: _____

_____

_____

PROBLEM 9.7A or 9.7B

_____

_____

GENERAL JOURNAL   PAGE _____

	DATE	DESCRIPTION	POST. REF.	DEBIT	CREDIT	
1						1
2						2
3						3
4						4
5						5
6						6
7						7
8						8
9						9
10						10
11						11
12						12
13						13

Analyze: _____

_____

PROBLEM 9.8A or 9.8B

PROBLEM 9.8A or 9.8B (continued)

GENERAL JOURNAL   PAGE _____

	DATE		DESCRIPTION	POST. REF.	DEBIT	CREDIT	
1							1
2							2
3							3
4							4
5							5
6							6
7							7
8							8
9							9
10							10
11							11
12							12
13							13
14							14
15							15
16							16
17							17
18							18
19							19
20							20
21							21
22							22
23							23
24							24
25							25
26							26
27							27
28							28

Analyze: _____

_____

_____

CRITICAL THINKING PROBLEM 9.1

SALES JOURNAL

PAGE _____

	DATE	SALES SLIP NO.	CUSTOMER'S NAME	POST. REF.	ACCOUNTS RECEIVABLE DEBIT	SALES TAX PAYABLE CREDIT	SALES CREDIT	
1								1
2								2
3								3
4								4
5								5
6								6
7								7
8								8
9								9
10								10
11								11
12								12
13								13
14								14
15								15
16								16

PURCHASES JOURNAL

PAGE _____

DATE	PURCHASED FROM	INVOICE NUMBER	INVOICE DATE	TERMS	POST. REF.	ACCOUNTS PAYABLE CREDIT	PURCHASES DEBIT	FREIGHT IN DEBIT

CRITICAL THINKING PROBLEM 9.1 (continued)

GENERAL JOURNAL   PAGE _____

	DATE		DESCRIPTION	POST. REF.	DEBIT	CREDIT	
1							1
2							2
3							3
4							4
5							5
6							6
7							7
8							8
9							9
10							10
11							11
12							12
13							13
14							14
15							15
16							16
17							17
18							18
19							19
20							20
21							21
22							22
23							23
24							24
25							25
26							26
27							27
28							28
29							29
30							30
31							31
32							32
33							33
34							34
35							35
36							36
37							37

CRITICAL THINKING PROBLEM 9.1 (continued)

CASH RECEIPTS JOURNAL

PAGE ____

DATE	DESCRIPTION	POST. REF.	ACCOUNTS RECEIVABLE CREDIT	SALES TAX PAYABLE CREDIT	SALES CREDIT	OTHER ACCOUNTS CREDIT			CASH DEBIT
						ACCOUNT NAME	POST. REF.	AMOUNT	

CRITICAL THINKING PROBLEM 9.1 (continued)

CASH PAYMENTS JOURNAL

DATE	CK. NO.	DESCRIPTION	POST. REF.	ACCOUNTS PAYABLE DEBIT	OTHER ACCOUNTS DEBIT			PURCHASES DISCOUNTS CREDIT	CASH CREDIT
					ACCOUNT NAME	POST. REF.	AMOUNT		

CRITICAL THINKING PROBLEM 9.1 (continued)

GENERAL LEDGER

ACCOUNT _____ ACCOUNT NO. _____

DATE	DESCRIPTION	POST. REF.	DEBIT	CREDIT	BALANCE	
					DEBIT	CREDIT

ACCOUNT _____ ACCOUNT NO. _____

DATE	DESCRIPTION	POST. REF.	DEBIT	CREDIT	BALANCE	
					DEBIT	CREDIT

ACCOUNT _____ ACCOUNT NO. _____

DATE	DESCRIPTION	POST. REF.	DEBIT	CREDIT	BALANCE	
					DEBIT	CREDIT

ACCOUNT _____ ACCOUNT NO. _____

DATE	DESCRIPTION	POST. REF.	DEBIT	CREDIT	BALANCE	
					DEBIT	CREDIT

ACCOUNT _____ ACCOUNT NO. _____

DATE	DESCRIPTION	POST. REF.	DEBIT	CREDIT	BALANCE	
					DEBIT	CREDIT

ACCOUNT _____ ACCOUNT NO. _____

DATE	DESCRIPTION	POST. REF.	DEBIT	CREDIT	BALANCE	
					DEBIT	CREDIT

CRITICAL THINKING PROBLEM 9.1 (continued)

GENERAL LEDGER

ACCOUNT _____ ACCOUNT NO. _____

DATE	DESCRIPTION	POST. REF.	DEBIT	CREDIT	BALANCE DEBIT	BALANCE CREDIT

ACCOUNT _____ ACCOUNT NO. _____

DATE	DESCRIPTION	POST. REF.	DEBIT	CREDIT	BALANCE DEBIT	BALANCE CREDIT

ACCOUNT _____ ACCOUNT NO. _____

DATE	DESCRIPTION	POST. REF.	DEBIT	CREDIT	BALANCE DEBIT	BALANCE CREDIT

ACCOUNT _____ ACCOUNT NO. _____

DATE	DESCRIPTION	POST. REF.	DEBIT	CREDIT	BALANCE DEBIT	BALANCE CREDIT

ACCOUNT _____ ACCOUNT NO. _____

DATE	DESCRIPTION	POST. REF.	DEBIT	CREDIT	BALANCE DEBIT	BALANCE CREDIT

CRITICAL THINKING PROBLEM 9.1 (continued)

GENERAL LEDGER

ACCOUNT _____ ACCOUNT NO. _____

DATE	DESCRIPTION	POST. REF.	DEBIT	CREDIT	BALANCE	
					DEBIT	CREDIT

ACCOUNT _____ ACCOUNT NO. _____

DATE	DESCRIPTION	POST. REF.	DEBIT	CREDIT	BALANCE	
					DEBIT	CREDIT

ACCOUNT _____ ACCOUNT NO. _____

DATE	DESCRIPTION	POST. REF.	DEBIT	CREDIT	BALANCE	
					DEBIT	CREDIT

ACCOUNT _____ ACCOUNT NO. _____

DATE	DESCRIPTION	POST. REF.	DEBIT	CREDIT	BALANCE	
					DEBIT	CREDIT

ACCOUNT _____ ACCOUNT NO. _____

DATE	DESCRIPTION	POST. REF.	DEBIT	CREDIT	BALANCE	
					DEBIT	CREDIT

CRITICAL THINKING PROBLEM 9.1 (continued)

GENERAL LEDGER

ACCOUNT _____ ACCOUNT NO. _____

DATE	DESCRIPTION	POST. REF.	DEBIT	CREDIT	BALANCE	
					DEBIT	CREDIT

ACCOUNT _____ ACCOUNT NO. _____

DATE	DESCRIPTION	POST. REF.	DEBIT	CREDIT	BALANCE	
					DEBIT	CREDIT

ACCOUNT _____ ACCOUNT NO. _____

DATE	DESCRIPTION	POST. REF.	DEBIT	CREDIT	BALANCE	
					DEBIT	CREDIT

ACCOUNTS RECEIVABLE SUBSIDIARY LEDGER

NAME _____ TERMS _____

DATE	DESCRIPTION	POST. REF.	DEBIT	CREDIT	BALANCE

NAME _____ TERMS _____

DATE	DESCRIPTION	POST. REF.	DEBIT	CREDIT	BALANCE

CRITICAL THINKING PROBLEM 9.1 (continued)

ACCOUNTS RECEIVABLE SUBSIDIARY LEDGER

NAME _____ TERMS _____

DATE	DESCRIPTION	POST. REF.	DEBIT	CREDIT	BALANCE

NAME _____ TERMS _____

DATE	DESCRIPTION	POST. REF.	DEBIT	CREDIT	BALANCE

NAME _____ TERMS _____

DATE	DESCRIPTION	POST. REF.	DEBIT	CREDIT	BALANCE

NAME _____ TERMS _____

DATE	DESCRIPTION	POST. REF.	DEBIT	CREDIT	BALANCE

NAME _____ TERMS _____

DATE	DESCRIPTION	POST. REF.	DEBIT	CREDIT	BALANCE

CRITICAL THINKING PROBLEM 9.1 (continued)

_____

_____

ACCOUNTS PAYABLE SUBSIDIARY LEDGER

NAME _____ TERMS _____

DATE	DESCRIPTION	POST. REF.	DEBIT	CREDIT	BALANCE

NAME _____ TERMS _____

DATE	DESCRIPTION	POST. REF.	DEBIT	CREDIT	BALANCE

NAME _____ TERMS _____

DATE	DESCRIPTION	POST. REF.	DEBIT	CREDIT	BALANCE

NAME _____ TERMS _____

DATE	DESCRIPTION	POST. REF.	DEBIT	CREDIT	BALANCE

CRITICAL THINKING PROBLEM 9.1 (continued)

NAME _____ TERMS _____

DATE	DESCRIPTION	POST. REF.	DEBIT	CREDIT	BALANCE

NAME _____ TERMS _____

DATE	DESCRIPTION	POST. REF.	DEBIT	CREDIT	BALANCE

ACCOUNTS PAYABLE SUBSIDIARY LEDGER

NAME _____ TERMS _____

DATE	DESCRIPTION	POST. REF.	DEBIT	CREDIT	BALANCE

Analyze: _____
_____

CRITICAL THINKING PROBLEM 9.2

CRITICAL THINKING PROBLEM 9.2 (continued)

_____

_____

_____

_____

_____

_____

_____

_____

_____

_____

_____

_____

_____

_____

_____

_____

_____

_____

_____

_____

_____

_____

_____

_____

_____

_____

Chapter 9 Practice Test Answer Key

Part A True-False		Part B Matching
1. T	13. T	1. g
2. T	14. F	2. h
3. T	15. T	3. f
4. T	16. F	4. a
5. F	17. T	5. d
6. F	18. T	6. b
7. F	19. T	7. c
8. T	20. F	8. e
9. F	21. T	9. i
10. F	22. F	10. j
11. T	23. F	11. k
12. F		12. l
		13. m

CHAPTER 10

Payroll Computations, Records, and Payment

STUDY GUIDE

Understanding the Chapter

Objectives	**1.** Explain the major federal laws relating to employee earnings and withholding. **2.** Compute gross earnings of employees. **3.** Determine employee deductions for social security taxes. **4.** Determine employee deductions for Medicare taxes. **5.** Determine employee deductions for income taxes. **6.** Enter gross earnings, deductions, and net pay in the payroll register. **7.** Journalize payroll transactions in the general journal. **8.** Maintain an earnings record for each employee. **9.** Define the accounting terms new to this chapter.
Reading Assignment	Read Chapter 10 in the textbook. Complete the Section Self Review as you finish reading each section of the chapter, and the Comprehensive Self Review at the end of the chapter. Refer to the Chapter 10 Glossary or to the Glossary at the end of the book to find definitions for terms that are not familiar to you.

Activities

❏ **Thinking Critically**	Answer the *Thinking Critically* questions for H&R Block and Managerial Implications.
❏ **Discussion Questions**	Answer each assigned review question in Chapter 10.
❏ **Exercises**	Complete each assigned exercise in Chapter 10. Use the forms provided in this SGWP. The objectives covered by an exercise are given after the exercise number. If you need help with an exercise, review the portion of the chapter related to the objective(s) covered.
❏ **Problems A/B**	Complete each assigned problem in Chapter 10. Use the forms provided in this SGWP. The objectives covered by a problem are given after the problem number. If you need help with a problem, review the portion of the chapter related to the objective(s) covered.
❏ **Critical Thinking Problems**	Complete the critical thinking problems as assigned. Use the forms provided in this SGWP.
❏ **Business Connections**	Complete the Business Connections activities as assigned to gain a deeper understanding of Chapter 10 concepts.

Practice Tests

Complete the Practice Tests, which cover the main points in your reading assignment. Compare your answers with those in the Practice Test Answer Key for Chapter 10 at the end of this chapter. If you have answered any questions incorrectly, review the related section of the text.

Part A True-False *For each of the following statements, circle T in the answer column if the statement is true or F if the statement is false.*

T   F   1. The Fair Labor Standards Act fixes a minimum wage for supervisory employees paid a monthly salary.

T   F   2. Payroll taxes apply to salaries and wages paid to employees and to amounts paid independent contractors.

T   F   3. Employees can choose whether they want to be covered by the social security laws.

T   F   4. Most employers determine the amount of income tax to be withheld from the employee's pay by using withholding tables.

T   F   5. The state unemployment tax rate can be reduced by the rate charged by the federal government in the federal unemployment tax program.

T   F   6. The employee's marital status, number of exemptions, earnings for the pay period, and length of pay period are all factors in determining the amount of social security tax to be withheld.

T   F   7. The employer is required to contribute the same amount of federal unemployment tax as the amount withheld from the employee's earnings.

T   F   8. The Medicare tax is included in the social security tax (OASDI).

T   F   9. The workers' compensation program is a federal program.

T   F   10. The payroll register provides all the information required to make a general journal entry to record the payroll.

T   F   11. An employee worked 44 hours during the week. Her regular hourly pay is $10 per hour. Her gross pay for the week is $440.00.

T   F   12. A company hires Charles Alexander, CPA, to prepare monthly financial statements. Alexander comes to the company's office, reviews source documents, and later returns the statements. He would be classified as an employee.

Part B Matching

For each numbered item, choose the matching term from the box and write the identifying letter in the answer column.

_____ 1. A record for each employee showing the person's earnings and deductions for the period, along with cumulative data.

_____ 2. Deductions to pay for medical benefits for retired persons.

_____ 3. A tax levied on the employer to provide benefits to employees who lose their jobs.

_____ 4. A government publication containing withholding tables for employee taxes.

_____ 5. Wages before deductions.

_____ 6. Wages paid in a year above the base amount subject to a tax.

_____ 7. A columnar record that shows each employee's earnings, deductions, and net pay.

_____ 8. Time worked in excess of 40 hours per week.

_____ 9. Provides for funding of retirement and disability benefits.

_____ 10. The form that employees file in order to claim the number of allowances to which they are entitled.

a. Employee earnings record

b. Payroll register

c. Exempt wages

d. Workers' compensation insurance

e. Overtime

f. Circular E

g. Medicare premiums

h. Unemployment tax

i. Federal Insurance Contributions Act

j. Employee's Withholding Allowance Certificate Form W4

k. Gross pay

Demonstration Problem

HR4u Consulting Company pays its employees monthly. Payments made by the company on November 30, 2016, follow. Cumulative amounts paid to the persons named prior to November 30 are also given.

1. Alexia Arciero, President, gross monthly salary of $17,000; gross earnings prior to November 30, $170,000.

2. Virginia Richey, Vice President, gross monthly salary of $14,000; gross earnings paid prior to November 30, $140,000.

3. Michael Price, independent accountant who audits the company's accounts, $17,500; gross amounts paid prior to November 30, $5,000.

4. Evelyn Wu, Treasurer, gross monthly salary of $10,060; gross earnings prior to November 30, $100,000.

5. Payment to Hankins Research Services for monthly services of Robert Hankins, a tax consultant, $7,000; amount paid to Hankins Research Services prior to November 30, $24,000.

Instructions

1. Use an earnings ceiling of $113,700, and a tax rate of 6.2 percent for social security taxes and a tax rate of 1.45 percent on all earnings for medicare taxes. Prepare a schedule showing:

   a. Each employee's cumulative earnings prior to November 30.

   b. Each employee's gross earnings for November.

   c. The amounts to be withheld for each payroll tax from each employee's earnings; the employee's income tax withholdings are Arciero, $5,500; Richey, $3,250; Wu, $1,250.

   d. The net amount due each employee.

   e. The total gross earnings, the total of each payroll tax deduction, and the total net amount payable to employees.

2. Give the general journal entry to record the company's payroll on November 30. Use journal page 34. Omit description.

3. Give the general journal entry to record payments to employees on November 30.

SOLUTION

EARNINGS SCHEDULE

EMPLOYEE NAME	CUMULATIVE EARNINGS	MONTHLY PAY	SOCIAL SECURITY	MEDICARE	EMPLOYEE INCOME TAX WITHHOLDING	NET PAY
John Arciero	$170,000.00	$17,000.00	—	$246.50	$5,500.00	$11,253.50
Virginia Richey	140,000.00	14,000.00	—	203.00	3,250.00	10,547.00
Evelyn Wu	100,000.00	10,000.00	620.00	145.00	1,250.00	7,985.00
Totals	$410,000.00	$41,000.00	$620.00	$594.50	$10,000.00	$29,785.50

Michael Price and Robert Hankins are not employees of HR4u Consulting Company.

GENERAL JOURNAL   PAGE 34

	DATE		DESCRIPTION	POST. REF.	DEBIT	CREDIT	
1	2016						1
2	Nov.	30	Salaries Expense		41 000 00		2
3			Social Security Tax Payable			620 00	3
4			Medicare Tax Payable			594 50	4
5			Employee Income Tax Payable			10 000 00	5
6			Salaries Payable			29 785 50	6
7							7
8		30	Salaries Payable		29 785 50		8
9			Cash			29 785 50	9
10							10

WORKING PAPERS

EXERCISE 10.1

EMPLOYEE NO.	HOURLY RATE	HOURS WORKED	GROSS EARNINGS
_____	_____	_____	_____
_____	_____	_____	_____
_____	_____	_____	_____
_____	_____	_____	_____

EXERCISE 10.2

HOURLY RATE	OVERTIME RATE	REGULAR HOURS WORKED	OVERTIME HOURS WORKED	REGULAR PAY	OVERTIME PAY	GROSS PAY
_____	_____	_____	_____	_____	_____	_____
_____	_____	_____	_____	_____	_____	_____
_____	_____	_____	_____	_____	_____	_____
_____	_____	_____	_____	_____	_____	_____

EXERCISE 10.3

EMPLOYEE NO.	DECEMBER SALARY	YEAR TO DATE EARNINGS THROUGH NOVEMBER 30	SOC. SEC. TAXABLE EARNINGS-DECEMBER	SOCIAL SECURITY TAX 6.20%
_____	_____	_____	_____	_____
_____	_____	_____	_____	_____
_____	_____	_____	_____	_____
_____	_____	_____	_____	_____

EXERCISE 10.4

EMPLOYEE NO.	DECEMBER SALARY	MEDICARE TAXABLE EARNINGS-DECEMBER	MEDICARE TAX 1.45%
_____	_____	_____	_____
_____	_____	_____	_____
_____	_____	_____	_____
_____	_____	_____	_____

EXERCISE 10.5

EMPLOYEE NO.	MARITAL STATUS	WITHHOLDING ALLOWANCES	WEEKLY SALARY	INCOME TAX WITHHOLDING
_____	_____	_____	_____	_____
_____	_____	_____	_____	_____
_____	_____	_____	_____	_____
_____	_____	_____	_____	_____

EXERCISE 10.6

GENERAL JOURNAL   PAGE _____

	DATE	DESCRIPTION	POST. REF.	DEBIT	CREDIT	
1						1
2						2
3						3
4						4
5						5
6						6
7						7
8						8
9						9
10						10
11						11
12						12
13						13
14						14
15						15

EXERCISE 10.7

GENERAL JOURNAL   PAGE _____

	DATE	DESCRIPTION	POST. REF.	DEBIT	CREDIT	
1						1
2						2
3						3
4						4
5						5
6						6
7						7
8						8
9						9
10						10
11						11
12						12
13						13
14						14
15						15

PROBLEM 10.1A or 10.1B

EMPLOYEE NO.	REGULAR HOURS, HOURLY RATE	HOURS WORKED	REGULAR TIME EARNINGS	OVERTIME EARNINGS	GROSS EARNINGS
_____	_____	_____	_____	_____	_____
_____	_____	_____	_____	_____	_____
_____	_____	_____	_____	_____	_____

Gross Pay _____

Social Security Tax _____

Medicare Tax _____

Income Tax Withholding _____

Health & Disability _____

Charitable Contribution _____

Savings _____

Net Pay _____

GENERAL JOURNAL

PAGE _____

	DATE	DESCRIPTION	POST. REF.	DEBIT	CREDIT	
1						1
2						2
3						3
4						4
5						5

Analyze: _____

_____

_____

_____

_____

_____

_____

PROBLEM 10.2A or 10.2B

PAYROLL REGISTER

WEEK BEGINNING _____ AND ENDING _____ PAID _____

NAME	NO. OF ALLOW.	MARITAL STATUS	CUMULATIVE EARNINGS	NO. OF HRS.	RATE	EARNINGS			CUMULATIVE EARNINGS
						REGULAR TIME EARNINGS	OVERTIME EARNINGS	GROSS AMOUNT	

	TAXABLE WAGES		DEDUCTIONS					DISTRIBUTION	
	SOCIAL SECURITY	MEDICARE	FUTA	SOCIAL SECURITY	MEDICARE	INCOME TAX	NET AMOUNT	CHECK NO.	WAGES EXPENSE

PROBLEM 10.2A or 10.2B (continued)

GENERAL JOURNAL

PAGE _____

	DATE	DESCRIPTION	POST. REF.	DEBIT	CREDIT	
1						1
2						2
3						3
4						4
5						5
6						6
7						7
8						8
9						9
10						10
11						11
12						12
13						13
14						14
15						15
16						16
17						17
18						18
19						19
20						20
21						21
22						22
23						23
24						24
25						25
26						26
27						27
28						28
29						29
30						30
31						31
32						32
33						33
34						34

Analyze: _____

_____

PROBLEM 10.3A or 10.3B

PAYROLL REGISTER   WEEK BEGINNING

NAME	NO. OF ALLOW.	MARITAL STATUS	CUMULATIVE EARNINGS	NO. OF HRS.	RATE	EARNINGS			CUMULATIVE EARNINGS
						REGULAR TIME EARNINGS	OVERTIME EARNINGS	GROSS AMOUNT	

AND ENDING   PAID

TAXABLE WAGES		DEDUCTIONS					NET AMOUNT	CHECK NO.	DISTRIBUTION	
SOCIAL SECURITY	MEDICARE	FUTA	SOCIAL SECURITY	MEDICARE	INCOME TAX				OFFICE WAGES	DELIVERY WAGES

PROBLEM 10.3A or 10.3B (continued)

GENERAL JOURNAL

PAGE _____

	DATE		DESCRIPTION	POST. REF.	DEBIT	CREDIT	
1							1
2							2
3							3
4							4
5							5
6							6
7							7
8							8
9							9
10							10
11							11
12							12
13							13
14							14
15							15
16							16
17							17
18							18
19							19
20							20
21							21
22							22
23							23
24							24
25							25
26							26
27							27
28							28
29							29
30							30
31							31
32							32
33							33
34							34

Analyze: _____

_____

PROBLEM 10.4A or 10.4B

EMPLOYEE NAME	CUMULATIVE EARNINGS	MONTHLY PAY	SOCIAL SECURITY	MEDICARE	EMPLOYEE INCOME TAX WITHHOLDING	NET PAY
Totals						

GENERAL JOURNAL

PAGE _____

	DATE	DESCRIPTION	POST. REF.	DEBIT	CREDIT	
1						1
2						2
3						3
4						4
5						5
6						6
7						7
8						8
9						9
10						10
11						11
12						12
13						13
14						14
15						15
16						16
17						17
18						18
19						19
20						20
21						21
22						22
23						23
24						24
25						25
26						26

Analyze: _____

_____

CRITICAL THINKING PROBLEM 10.1

EMPLOYEE NAME	CUMULATIVE EARNINGS	MONTHLY PAY	SOCIAL SECURITY	MEDICARE	EMPLOYEE INCOME TAX WITHHOLDING	NET PAY

GENERAL JOURNAL

PAGE _____

	DATE		DESCRIPTION	POST. REF.	DEBIT	CREDIT	
1							1
2							2
3							3
4							4
5							5
6							6
7							7
8							8
9							9
10							10
11							11
12							12
13							13
14							14
15							15

Analyze: _____

_____

CRITICAL THINKING PROBLEM 10.2

_____

_____

_____

_____

_____

_____

_____

_____

_____

_____

_____

_____

_____

_____

_____

_____

_____

_____

_____

_____

_____

_____

_____

_____

_____

_____

_____

Chapter 10 Practice Test Answer Key

Part A True-False	Part B Matching
1. F	1. a
2. F	2. g
3. F	3. h
4. T	4. f
5. F	5. k
6. F	6. c
7. F	7. b
8. F	8. e
9. F	9. i
10. T	10. j
11. F	
12. F	

CHAPTER 11

Payroll Taxes, Deposits, and Reports

STUDY GUIDE

Understanding the Chapter

Objectives

1. Explain how and when payroll taxes are paid to the government. 2. Compute and record the employer's social security and Medicare taxes. 3. Record deposit of social security, Medicare, and employee income taxes. 4. Prepare an Employer's Quarterly Federal Tax Return, Form 941. 5. Prepare Wage and Tax Statement (Form W-2) and Annual Transmittal of Wage and Tax Statements (Form W-3). 6. Compute and record liability for federal and state unemployment taxes and record payment of the taxes. 7. Prepare an Employer's Federal Unemployment Tax Return, Form 940 or 940-EZ. 8. Compute and record workers' compensation insurance premiums. 9. Define the accounting terms new to this chapter.

Reading Assignment

Read Chapter 11 in the textbook. Complete the textbook Section Self Review as you finish reading each section of the chapter, and Comprehensive Self Review at the end of the chapter. Refer to the Chapter 11 Glossary or to the Glossary at the end of the book to find definitions for terms that are not familiar to you.

Activities

❏ **Thinking Critically**
Answer the *Thinking Critically* questions for Marek Brothers Systems, Inc. and Resorts and Managerial Implications.

❏ **Discussion Questions**
Answer each assigned discussion question in Chapter 11.

❏ **Exercises**
Complete each assigned exercise in Chapter 11. Use the forms provided in this SGWP. The objectives covered by an exercise are given after the exercise number. If you need help with an exercise, review the portion of the chapter related to the objective(s) covered.

❏ **Problems A/B**
Complete each assigned problem in Chapter 11. Use the forms provided in this SGWP. The objectives covered by a problem are given after the problem number. If you need help with a problem, review the portion of the chapter related to the objective(s) covered.

❏ **Critical Thinking Problems**
Complete the critical thinking problems as assigned. Use the forms provided in this SGWP.

❏ **Business Connections**
Complete the Business Connections activities as assigned to gain a deeper understanding of Chapter 11 concepts.

Practice Tests

Complete the Practice Tests, which cover the main points in your reading assignment. Compare your answers with those in the Practice Test Answer Key for Chapter 11 at the end of this chapter. If you have answered any questions incorrectly, review the related section of the text.

Part A True-False

For each of the following statements, circle T in the answer column if the statement is true or F if the statement is false.

T F **1.** Employers with a small number of employees are frequently required to deposit the entire amount of estimated workers' compensation insurance premiums early in the year.

T F **2.** The credit against the federal unemployment tax is the amount actually paid to the state under its unemployment compensation insurance program.

T F **3.** The premium on workers' compensation insurance is based on the federal unemployment tax.

T F **4.** Premiums on workers' compensation insurance vary with the type of work performed by employees.

T F **5.** The federal unemployment tax for the year is based on an audit of the payroll for the year.

T F **6.** Under a typical state plan, the federal government actually receives 0.8 percent of the taxable wages because the employer is allowed credits for payments made to the state.

T F **7.** The federal government grants a lower federal unemployment rate under an experience rating system to those employers who provide stable employment.

T F **8.** Most states allow a credit against the FUTA for amounts paid to the federal government as SUTA.

T F **9.** The employer's payroll taxes are usually recorded at the end of each payroll period, even though the cash will not be paid out until later.

T F **10.** A business firm pays income tax withholding at the same rate and on the same taxable wages as employees.

T F **11.** During the month immediately following the close of each calendar quarter, an employer is required to file a quarterly tax report and pay in or deposit any balance owed for social security and Medicare taxes and employees' income tax withheld.

T F **12.** On each date of payment of an employee's wages, the employer must provide the employee with a statement, on Form W-2, of earnings and taxes withheld.

T F **13.** Employees' individual earnings records provide much of the information needed to prepare the Employer's Quarterly Federal Tax Return, Form 941.

T F **14.** Only the amount of each employee's earnings up to $7,000 each year is subject to the social security tax.

T F **15.** Payments of social security tax, Medicare tax, and employee income tax withheld may be deposited, without penalty, in an authorized depository at any time up to January 31 of the following year.

T F **16.** The employee must attach a Form W-3 to his or her federal income tax return.

T F **17.** Each employer subject to the Federal Unemployment Compensation Tax Act must file an annual return on Form 940 by January 15 of the following year.

T F **18.** Social security taxes are paid by the employer but not the employee.

Part B Matching

For each number item, choose the matching term from the box and write the identifying letter in the answer column.

_____	**1.**	A tax borne equally by the employer and employee.
_____	**2.**	A tax paid solely by the employer.
_____	**3.**	An IRS publication containing tax rates and other information about payroll taxes.
_____	**4.**	Plan providing benefits to employees who are injured or become ill on the job.
_____	**5.**	A plan under which the SUTA is adjusted to reflect the unemployment experience of the employer.
_____	**6.**	A yearly form sent to the U.S. government summarizing earnings and payroll taxes withheld for the year.
_____	**7.**	A statement of earnings and deductions for each employee.
_____	**8.**	A deposit "coupon" accompanying the employer's deposit of taxes in a commercial bank.
_____	**9.**	An annual report to the federal government summarizing the employer's unemployment compensation tax for the year.
_____	**10.**	A quarterly report to the federal government summarizing taxable wages and payroll taxes due for the quarter.

a. Workers' compensation

b. Form 8109

c. Form 941

d. Form 940

e. Form W-3

f. Form W-2

g. Experience rating system

h. Publication 15, Circular E

i. Federal unemployment tax

j. Medicare tax

Demonstration Problem

The payroll register of the USA Printing and Copy Center showed employee earnings of $16,000 for the month ended January 31, 2016. Employee income tax withholding was $2,400. Use a social security rate of 6.2%, Medicare rate of 1.45%, FUTA rate of 0.6%, and SUTA rate of 5.4%. Assure all earnings are subject to these taxes.

Instructions

1. Compute the employees' social security and Medicare taxes.
2. Record the payroll for January in the general journal, page 3.
3. Compute the employer's payroll taxes for the period.
4. Prepare a general journal entry to record the employer's payroll taxes for the period.
5. Prepare a general journal entry to record the February 4 deposit of the social security, Medicare, and employee income taxes for the month.

SOLUTION

CALCULATION OF EMPLOYEE TAXES

Social security: 0.062 × $16,000	$992.00
Medicare: 0.0145 × $16,000	232.00
	$1,224.00

CALCULATION OF EMPLOYER TAXES

Social security: 0.062 × $16,000	$992.00
Medicare: 0.0145 × $16,000	232.00
FUTA: 0.006 × $16,000	96.00
SUTA: 0.054 × $16,000	864.00
	$2,184.00

SOLUTION (continued)

GENERAL JOURNAL   PAGE ___3___

	DATE		DESCRIPTION	POST. REF.	DEBIT	CREDIT	
1	2016						1
2	Jan.	31	**Salaries Expense**		16 0 0 0 00		2
3			**Social Security Tax Payable**			9 9 2 00	3
4			**Medicare Tax Payable**			2 3 2 00	4
5			**Employee Income Tax Payable**			2 4 0 0 00	5
6			**Salaries Payable**			12 3 7 6 00	6
7			**Payroll for January**				7
8							8
9		31	**Payroll Tax Expense**		2 1 8 4 00		9
10			**Social Security Tax Payable**			9 9 2 00	10
11			**Medicare Tax Payable**			2 3 2 00	11
12			**Federal Unemployment Tax Payable**			9 6 00	12
13			**State Unemployment Tax Payable**			8 6 4 00	13
14			**Payroll for January**				14
15							15
16	Feb.	4	**Social Security Tax Payable**		1 9 8 4 00		16
17			**Medicare Tax Payable**		4 6 4 00		17
18			**Employee Income Tax Payable**		2 4 0 0 00		18
19			**Cash**			4 8 4 8 00	19
20			**Deposit of payroll taxes withholding**				20
21							21
22							22
23							23
24							24
25							25
26							26
27							27
28							28
29							29
30							30
31							31
32							32
33							33
34							34
35							35
36							36
37							37
38							38

WORKING PAPERS

EXERCISE 11.1

_____
_____
_____
_____
_____

EXERCISE 11.2

GENERAL JOURNAL

PAGE _____

	DATE		DESCRIPTION	POST. REF.	DEBIT	CREDIT	
1							1
2							2
3							3
4							4
5							5
6							6
7							7

EXERCISE 11.3

TAX	BASE	RATE	AMOUNT
_____	_____	_____	_____
_____	_____	_____	_____
_____	_____	_____	_____
_____	_____	_____	_____

EXERCISE 11.4

GENERAL JOURNAL

PAGE _____

	DATE		DESCRIPTION	POST. REF.	DEBIT	CREDIT	
1							1
2							2
3							3
4							4
5							5
6							6
7							7

EXERCISE 11.5

_____

_____

_____

EXERCISE 11.6

GENERAL JOURNAL   PAGE _____

	DATE		DESCRIPTION	POST. REF.	DEBIT	CREDIT	
1							1
2							2
3							3
4							4
5							5
6							6
7							7

EXERCISE 11.7

_____

_____

_____

_____

EXERCISE 11.8

WORK CLASSIFICATION	ESTIMATED EARNINGS	RATE	ESTIMATED PREMIUM
_____	_____	_____	_____
_____	_____	_____	_____
_____	_____	_____	_____

PROBLEM 11.1A or 11.1B

TAX	BASE	RATE	AMOUNT
_____	_____	_____	_____
_____	_____	_____	_____
_____	_____	_____	_____
_____	_____	_____	_____
_____	_____	_____	_____

GENERAL JOURNAL

PAGE __28__

	DATE	DESCRIPTION	POST. REF.	DEBIT	CREDIT	
1						1
2						2
3						3
4						4
5						5
6						6
7						7
8						8
9						9
10						10
11						11
12						12

Analyze: _____

PROBLEM 11.2A or 11.2B

GENERAL JOURNAL   PAGE _____

	DATE		DESCRIPTION	POST. REF.	DEBIT	CREDIT	
1							1
2							2
3							3
4							4
5							5
6							6
7							7
8							8
9							9
10							10
11							11
12							12
13							13
14							14
15							15
16							16
17							17
18							18
19							19
20							20
21							21
22							22
23							23
24							24
25							25
26							26
27							27
28							28
29							29
30							30
31							31
32							32
33							33

Analyze: _____

_____

PROBLEM 11.3A or 11.3B

GENERAL JOURNAL   PAGE _____

	DATE		DESCRIPTION	POST. REF.	DEBIT	CREDIT	
1							1
2							2
3							3
4							4
5							5
6							6
7							7
8							8
9							9
10							10
11							11
12							12
13							13
14							14
15							15
16							16
17							17
18							18
19							19
20							20
21							21
22							22
23							23
24							24
25							25
26							26
27							27
28							28
29							29
30							30
31							31
32							32
33							33

Analyze: _____

_____

PROBLEM 11.3A or 11.3B (continued)

Form **941 for 2016:** Employer's Quarterly Federal Tax Return

Department of the Treasury — Internal Revenue Service

9901

OMB No. 1545-0029

Employer identification number ⬚⬚ – ⬚⬚⬚⬚⬚⬚⬚

Name (not your trade name) _____

Trade name (if any) _____

Address _____

Number   Street   Suite or room number

City   State   ZIP code

Report for this Quarter ...
(Check one.)

☐ **1:** January, February, March

☒ **2:** April, May, June

☐ **3:** July, August, September

☐ **4:** October, November, December

Read the separate instructions before you fill out this form. Please type or print within the boxes.

Part 1: Answer these questions for this quarter.

1 Number of employees who received wages, tips, or other compensation for the pay period including: *Mar. 16* (Quarter 1), *June 16* (Quarter 2), *Sept. 16* (Quarter 3), *Dec. 16* (Quarter 4) **1** ⬚

2 Wages, tips, and other compensation . . . . **2** ⬚

3 Total income tax withheld from wages, tips, and other compensation . . . . . **3** ⬚

4 If no wages, tips, and other compensation are subject to social security or Medicare tax . ☐ Check and go to line 6.

5 Taxable social security and Medicare wages and tips:

	Column 1		Column 2
5a Taxable social security wages	⬚	× .124 =	⬚
5b Taxable social security tips	⬚	× .124 =	⬚
5c Taxable Medicare wages & tips	⬚	× .029 =	⬚

5d Total social security and Medicare taxes (Column 2, lines 5a + 5b + 5c = line 5d) . **5d** ⬚

6 Total taxes before adjustments (lines 3 + 5d = line 6) . . . . **6** ⬚

7 Tax adjustments (If your answer is a negative number, write it in brackets.):

7a Current quarter's fractions of cents . . . . ⬚

7b Current quarter's sick pay . . . . ⬚

7c Current quarter's adjustments for tips and group-term life insurance ⬚

7d Current year's income tax withholding (Attach Form 941c) . . . ⬚

7e Prior quarters' social security and Medicare taxes (Attach Form 941c) ⬚

7f Special additions to federal income tax (reserved use) . . . . ⬚

7g Special additions to social security and Medicare (reserved use) ⬚

7h Total adjustments (Combine all amounts: lines 7a through 7g.) . . . . . **7h** ⬚

8 Total taxes after adjustments (Combine lines 6 and 7h.) . . . . **8** ⬚

9 Advance earned income credit (EIC) payments made to employees . . . . . . **9** ⬚

10 Total taxes after adjustment for advance EIC (lines 8 – 9 = line 10) . . . . . . **10** ⬚

11 Total deposits for this quarter, including overpayment applied from a prior quarter . **11** ⬚

12 Balance due (lines 10 – 11 = line 12) Make checks payable to the *United States Treasury* **12** ⬚

13 Overpayment (If line 11 is more than line 10, write the difference here.) ⬚ Check one ☐ Apply to next return.
☐ Send a refund.

Next ➡

For Privacy Act and Paperwork Reduction Act Notice, see the back of the Payment Voucher.   Cat. No. 17001Z   Form **941**

Name _____

PROBLEM 11.3A or 11.3B (continued)

9902

Name (not your trade name)	Employer identification number

Part 2: Tell us about your deposit schedule for this quarter.

If you are unsure about whether you are a monthly schedule depositor or a semiweekly schedule depositor, see *Pub. 15 (Circular E)*, section 11.

14 [ ] [ ] Write the state abbreviation for the state where you made your deposits OR write "MU" if you made your deposits in *multiple* states.

15 Check one: [ ] Line 10 is less than $2,500. Go to Part 3.

[ ] You were a monthly schedule depositor for the entire quarter. Fill out your tax liability for each month. Then go to Part 3.

Tax liability: Month 1 [_____ .]

Month 2 [_____ .]

Month 3 [_____ .]

Total [_____ .] Total must equal line 10.

[ ] You were a semiweekly schedule depositor for any part of this quarter. Fill out *Schedule B (Form 941): Report of Tax Liability for Semiweekly Schedule Depositors,* and attach it to this form.

Part 3: Tell us about your business. If a question does NOT apply to your business, leave it blank.

16 If your business has closed and you do not have to file returns in the future . . . . [ ] Check here, and

enter the final date you paid wages [/   /   ] .

17 If you are a seasonal employer and you do not have to file a return for every quarter of the year . [ ] Check here.

Part 4: May we contact your third-party designee?

Do you want to allow an employee, a paid tax preparer, or another person to discuss this return with the IRS? See the instructions for details.

[ ] Yes. Designee's name [_____]

Phone ([   ]) [   ] – [   ]   Personal Identification Number (PIN) [ ] [ ] [ ] [ ] [ ]

[ ] No.

Part 5: Sign here

Under penalties of perjury, I declare that I have examined this return, including accompanying schedules and statements, and to the best of my knowledge and belief, it is true, correct, and complete.

X

Sign your name here [_____]

Print name and title [_____]

Date [/   /   ]   Phone ([   ]) [   ] – [   ]

Part 6: For paid preparers only (optional)

Preparer's signature [_____]

Firm's name [_____]

Address [_____]   EIN [_____]

[_____]   ZIP code [_____]

Date [/   /   ]   Phone ([   ]) [   ] – [   ]   SSN/PTIN [_____]

[ ] Check if you are self-employed.

Form **941**

PROBLEM 11.4A or 11.4B

_____
_____
_____

GENERAL JOURNAL

PAGE _____

	DATE		DESCRIPTION	POST. REF.	DEBIT	CREDIT	
1							1
2							2
3							3
4							4
5							5
6							6
7							7
8							8
9							9
10							10
11							11
12							12
13							13
14							14
15							15
16							16
17							17
18							18
19							19
20							20
21							21
22							22
23							23
24							24
25							25
26							26
27							27
28							28
29							29

Analyze: _____

PROBLEM 11.5A or 11.5B

GENERAL JOURNAL

PAGE _____

	DATE		DESCRIPTION	POST. REF.	DEBIT	CREDIT	
1							1
2							2
3							3
4							4
5							5
6							6
7							7
8							8
9							9
10							10
11							11
12							12
13							13
14							14
15							15
16							16
17							17
18							18
19							19
20							20
21							21
22							22
23							23
24							24
25							25
26							26
27							27
28							28
29							29
30							30
31							31
32							32
33							33
34							34

Analyze: _____

_____

PROBLEM 11.5A or 11.5B (continued)

Form **940-EZ**	**Employer's Annual Federal** **Unemployment (FUTA) Tax Return**	OMB No. 1545-1110
Department of the Treasury Internal Revenue Service	► See the separate Instructions for Form 940-EZ for information on completing this form.	**2016**

		T
		FF
		FD
		FP
		I
		T

You must complete this section. ►	Name (as distinguished from trade name)	Calendar year
	Trade name, if any	Employer identification number (EIN)
	Address (number and street)	City, state, and ZIP code

Answer the questions under **Who May Use Form 940-EZ** on page 2. If you cannot use Form 940-EZ, you must use Form 940.

A   Enter the amount of contributions paid to your state unemployment fund (see the separate instructions) . . ► $ _____

B   (1) Enter the name of the state where you have to pay contributions . . . . ► _____

(2) Enter your state reporting number as shown on your state unemployment tax return ►

If you will not have to file returns in the future, check here (see **Who Must File** in separate instructions) **and complete and sign the return.** ► ☐

If this is an Amended Return, check here (see **Amended Returns** in the separate instructions) . . . . ► ☐

Part I   Taxable Wages and FUTA Tax

1	Total payments (including payments shown on lines 2 and 3) during the calendar year for services of employees	**1**	
2	Exempt payments. (Explain all exempt payments, attaching additional sheets if necessary.) ► _____ _____	**2**	
3	Payments of more than $7,000 for services. Enter only amounts over the first $7,000 paid to each employee **(see the separate instructions)**	**3**	
4	Add lines 2 and 3	**4**	
5	**Total taxable wages** (subtract line 4 from line 1) . . . . ►	**5**	
6	**FUTA tax.** Multiply the wages on line 5 by .006 and enter here. **(If the result is over $100, also complete Part II.)**	**6**	
7	Total FUTA tax deposited for the year, including any overpayment applied from a prior year . . . . ►	**7**	
8	**Balance due** (subtract line 7 from line 6). Pay to the "United States Treasury." . . . . . . ►	**8**	
	If you owe more than $100, see **Depositing FUTA tax** in the separate instructions.		
9	**Overpayment** (subtract line 6 from line 7). Check if it is to be: ☐ **Applied to next return** or ☐ **Refunded** ►	**9**	

Part II   Record of Quarterly Federal Unemployment Tax Liability (Do not include state liability.) Complete only if line 6 is over $100.

Quarter	First (Jan. 1 – Mar. 31)	Second (Apr. 1 – June 30)	Third (July 1 – Sept. 30)	Fourth (Oct. 1 – Dec. 31)	Total for year
Liability for quarter					

Third-Party Designee	Do you want to allow another person to discuss this return with the IRS (see the separate instructions)? ☐ **Yes.** Complete the following. ☐ **No**		
	Designee's name ►	Phone no. ► ( )	Personal identification number (PIN) ►

Under penalties of perjury, I declare that I have examined this return, including accompanying schedules and statements, and, to the best of my knowledge and belief, it is true, correct, and complete, and that no part of any payment made to a state unemployment fund claimed as a credit was, or is to be, deducted from the payments to employees.

Signature ► _____   Title (Owner, etc.) ► _____   Date ► _____

For Privacy Act and Paperwork Reduction Act Notice, see the separate instructions.   ▼ **DETACH HERE** ▼   Cat. No. 10983G   Form **940-EZ**

Form **940-V(EZ)**	**Payment Voucher**	OMB No. 1545-1110
Department of the Treasury Internal Revenue Service	Use this voucher only when making a payment with your return.	**2016**

Complete boxes 1, 2, and 3. Do not send cash, and do not staple your payment to this voucher. Make your check or money order payable to the "United States Treasury." Be sure to enter your employer identification number (EIN), "Form 940-EZ," and "2004" on your payment.

1 Enter your employer identification number (EIN).	**2** **Enter the amount of your payment.** ►	Dollars	Cents
	3 Enter your business name (individual name for sole proprietors).		
	Enter your address.		
	Enter your city, state, and ZIP code.		

PROBLEM 11.6A or 11.6B

WORK CLASSIFICATION	ESTIMATED EARNINGS	INSURANCE RATE	ESTIMATED PREMIUMS
_____	_____	_____	_____
_____	_____	_____	_____
_____	_____	_____	_____

WORK CLASSIFICATION	ACTUAL EARNINGS	INSURANCE RATE	ACTUAL PREMIUMS
_____	_____	_____	_____
_____	_____	_____	_____
_____	_____	_____	_____
_____	_____	_____	_____

PROBLEM 11.6A or 11.6B (continued)

GENERAL JOURNAL   PAGE _____

	DATE		DESCRIPTION	POST. REF.	DEBIT	CREDIT	
1							1
2							2
3							3
4							4
5							5
6							6
7							7
8							8
9							9
10							10
11							11
12							12
13							13
14							14
15							15
16							16
17							17
18							18
19							19

Analyze: _____

_____

CRITICAL THINKING PROBLEM 11.1

1. _____
   _____
   _____
   _____

2. **YEARLY COST—CURRENT SYSTEM**

   _____
   _____
   _____
   _____
   _____
   _____
   _____
   _____
   _____
   _____
   _____
   _____
   _____
   _____
   _____

CRITICAL THINKING PROBLEM 11.2

1. _____
   _____

2. _____
   _____

3. _____

4. _____
   _____

5. _____
   _____

Analyze: _____
   _____

CRITICAL THINKING PROBLEM 11.2 (continued)

YEARLY COST—PROPOSED SYSTEM

_____

_____

_____

_____

_____

_____

_____

_____

_____

_____

_____

_____

_____

_____

_____

_____

3. _____

_____

_____

_____

_____

Chapter 11 Practice Test Answer Key

Part A True-False		Part B Matching
1. T	10. F	1. j
2. F	11. T	2. i
3. F	12. F	3. h
4. T	13. T	4. a
5. F	14. F	5. g
6. T	15. F	6. e
7. F	16. F	7. f
8. F	17. F	8. b
9. T	18. F	9. d
		10. c

CHAPTER 12

Accruals, Deferrals, and the Worksheet

STUDY GUIDE

Understanding the Chapter

Objectives

1. Determine the adjustment for merchandise inventory and enter the adjustment on the worksheet. 2. Compute adjustments for accrued and prepaid expense items and enter the adjustments on the worksheet. 3. Compute adjustments for accrued and deferred income items and enter the adjustments on the worksheet. 4. Complete a ten-column worksheet. 5. Define the accounting terms new to this chapter.

Reading Assignment

Read Chapter 12 in the textbook. Complete the textbook Section Self Review as you finish reading each section of the chapter, and the Comprehensive Self Review at the end of the chapter. Refer to the Chapter 12 Glossary or to the Glossary at the end of the book to find definitions for terms that are not familiar to you.

Activities

❏ **Thinking Critically**

Answer the *Thinking Critically* questions for Urban Outfitters and Managerial Implications.

❏ **Discussion Questions**

Answer each assigned discussion question in Chapter 12.

❏ **Exercises**

Complete each assigned exercise in Chapter 12. Use the forms provided in this SGWP. The objectives covered by an exercise are given after the exercise number. If you need help with an exercise, review the portion of the chapter related to the objective(s) covered.

❏ **Problems A/B**

Complete each assigned problem in Chapter 12. Use the forms provided in this SGWP. The objectives covered by a problem are given after the problem number. If you need help with a problem, review the portion of the chapter related to the objective(s) covered.

❏ **Critical Thinking Problems**

Complete the critical thinking problems as assigned. Use the forms provided in this SGWP.

❏ **Business Connections**

Complete the Business Connections activities as assigned to gain a deeper understanding of Chapter 12 concepts.

Practice Tests

Complete the Practice Tests, which cover the main points in your reading assignment. Compare your answers with those in the Practice Test Answer Key for Chapter 12 at the end of this chapter. If you have answered any questions incorrectly, review the related section of the text.

Part A True-False   *For each of the following statements, circle T in the answer column if the statement is true or F if the statement is false.*

T F **1.** The Adjusted Trial Balance column of the worksheet tests only the arithmetic accuracy of the worksheet to that point in the worksheet and statement preparation process.

T F **2.** After the amounts shown in the Adjusted Trial Balance section have been extended, the difference between the total debits and total credits in the balance sheet section represents the net income or loss for the period.

T F **3.** The accountant completes the worksheet and prepares the financial statements as soon as all adjustments have been entered on the worksheet.

T F **4.** The net income for the business is entered as a debit entry in the Balance Sheet section and as a credit entry in the Income Statement section of the worksheet.

T F **5.** Office or store supplies that have been paid for in cash do not need any adjusting entries.

T F **6.** On the trial balance, the **Store Supplies** account shows a debit balance of $300. A physical count showed supplies on hand of $80. The adjusting entry includes a debit of $80 to the **Store Supplies Expense** account.

T F **7.** An adjustment for depreciation results in an entry debiting the **Depreciation Expense** account and crediting the **Equipment** account.

T F **8.** At the end of an accounting period, an adjustment is needed to record as an expense any part of the balance in an asset account that has been used up or has expired.

T F **9.** The unadjusted trial balance figures for accumulated depreciation accounts do not include depreciation for the current period.

T F **10.** The **Unearned Subscriptions Income** account will appear in the Liabilities section of the balance sheet.

T F **11.** In the "adjustments" column of the worksheet, the **Merchandise Inventory** is debited for the amount of ending inventory and credited for the amount of beginning inventory.

T F **12.** Under the accrual basis of accounting, purchases are recorded after the purchase has been paid.

T F **13.** The **Interest Expense** account must be adjusted if an interest-bearing note payable is outstanding at the end of the fiscal period and interest has not been paid on that date.

T F **14.** In most cases, **Prepaid Interest** will be classified in the Assets section on the balance sheet.

T F **15.** The entry to record accrued interest on notes payable is a debit to **Interest Expense** and a credit to **Interest Receivable.**

T F **16.** **Interest Receivable** is usually classified as a revenue account.

T F **17.** Deferred income has been earned but not recorded, while accrued income has been recorded but not earned.

T F **18.** Adjusting entries are recorded in the general journal after the worksheet and the financial statements are completed.

T F **19.** The beginning merchandise inventory does not appear in the Adjusted Trial Balance.

T F **20.** The **Drawing** account balance is extended to the Debit column in the Income Statement section.

T F **21.** The financial statements are prepared directly from the worksheet.

T F **22.** The statement of owner's equity should be prepared after the income statement is prepared.

T F **23.** In preparing financial statements, it is unnecessary to make adjustments for relatively small items because they are immaterial and will not affect the statements.

T F **24.** The accounts should be adjusted when preparing monthly or quarterly statements.

T F **25.** A prepaid expense incorrectly charged to expense in an accounting period results in an understatement of net income in that period and an overstatement of net income in the following period.

Part B Exercise *In each of the following independent cases give the general journal entry to adjust the accounts for the year on December 31, 2016. Omit the descriptions.*

1. Store supplies costing $1,600 were purchased during the year and were charged to the **Store Supplies** account. At the end of the year, supplies costing $200 were on hand.

GENERAL JOURNAL
PAGE _____

	DATE	DESCRIPTION	POST. REF.	DEBIT	CREDIT	
1						1
2						2

2. On December 1, 2016 the company gave a $5,000 note payable to a supplier. The note bears interest at 6 percent.

GENERAL JOURNAL
PAGE _____

	DATE	DESCRIPTION	POST. REF.	DEBIT	CREDIT	
1						1
2						2

3. On October 1, 2016, the company received a four-month, 8 percent note for $3,500 from settlement of an overdue account. No interest has been recorded on the note.

GENERAL JOURNAL
PAGE _____

	DATE	DESCRIPTION	POST. REF.	DEBIT	CREDIT	
1						1
2						2

4. On November 1, 2016, the company purchased a one-year insurance policy for $8,400. The amount was charged to **Prepaid Insurance.**

GENERAL JOURNAL
PAGE _____

	DATE	DESCRIPTION	POST. REF.	DEBIT	CREDIT	
1						1
2						2

5. During 2016, the Irvine Quakes minor league hockey team received $1,200,000 from the sale of season tickets for 20 home games. The Unearned Season Tickets Income account was credited upon receipt of the cash. As of December 31, 8 home games had been played.

GENERAL JOURNAL
PAGE _____

	DATE	DESCRIPTION	POST. REF.	DEBIT	CREDIT	
1						1
2						2

Demonstration Problem

The trial balance for Pietro's Imports on December 31, 2016, the end of its accounting period, is shown on the worksheet.

Instructions

1. Complete the worksheet for the year, using the following information:

   a-b. Ending merchandise inventory, $109,250.

   c. Uncollectible accounts expense, $2,900.

   d. Supplies on hand December 31, $2,780.

   e. Depreciation on store equipment, $8,100.

   f. Depreciation on office equipment, $5,875.

   g. Accrued sales salaries, $4,000; accrued office salaries, $750.

   h. Tax on accrued salaries: social security, $294.50; Medicare, $68.88.

2. Journalize the adjusting entries on page 16 of the general journal.

SOLUTION

Pietro's Imports
Worksheet
Year Ended December 31, 2016

ACCOUNT NAME	TRIAL BALANCE DEBIT	TRIAL BALANCE CREDIT	ADJUSTMENTS DEBIT	ADJUSTMENTS CREDIT	ADJUSTED TRIAL BALANCE DEBIT	ADJUSTED TRIAL BALANCE CREDIT	INCOME STATEMENT DEBIT	INCOME STATEMENT CREDIT	BALANCE SHEET DEBIT	BALANCE SHEET CREDIT
Cash	39,810.00				39,810.00				39,810.00	
Accounts Receivable	32,340.00				32,340.00				32,340.00	
Allowance for Doubtful Accounts		5,060.00		2,900.00		7,960.00				7,960.00
Merchandise Inventory	116,780.00		109,250.00	116,780.00	109,250.00				109,250.00	
Supplies	10,600.00			7,820.00	2,780.00				2,780.00	
Store Equipment	84,000.00				84,000.00				84,000.00	
Accum. Depr., Store Equip.		16,590.00		8,100.00		24,690.00				24,690.00
Office Equipment	25,700.00				25,700.00				25,700.00	
Accum. Depr., Office Equip.		7,033.00		5,875.00		12,908.00				12,908.00
Accounts Payable		22,560.00				22,560.00				22,560.00
Salaries Payable				4,750.00		4,750.00				4,750.00
Social Security Tax Payable				294.50		294.50				294.50
Medicare-Tax Payable				68.88		68.88				68.88
Pietro Canzone, Capital		230,764.00				230,764.00				230,764.00
Pietro Canzone, Drawing	26,000.00				26,000.00				26,000.00	
Income Summary			116,780.00	109,250.00	116,780.00	109,250.00	116,780.00	109,250.00		
Sales		424,642.00				424,642.00		424,642.00		
Sales Returns and Allowances	8,155.00				8,155.00		8,155.00			
Purchases	197,534.00				197,534.00		197,534.00			
Purchases Returns and Allowances		1,200.00				1,200.00		1,200.00		
Purchases Discounts		600.00				600.00		600.00		
Freight In	12,260.00				12,260.00		12,260.00			
Sales Salaries Expense	94,580.00		4,000.00		98,580.00		98,580.00			
Rent Expense	31,000.00				31,000.00		31,000.00			
Advertising Expense	12,045.00				12,045.00		12,045.00			
Supplies Expense			7,820.00		7,820.00		7,820.00			
Depreciation Exp., Store Equip.			8,100.00		8,100.00		8,100.00			
Office Salaries Expense	17,645.00		750.00		18,395.00		18,395.00			
Payroll Taxes Expense			363.38		363.38		363.38			
Depreciation Exp., Office Equip.			5,875.00		5,875.00		5,875.00			
Uncollectible Accounts Expense			2,900.00		2,900.00		2,900.00			
	708,449.00	708,449.00	255,838.38	255,838.38	839,687.38	839,687.38	519,807.38	535,692.00	319,880.00	303,995.38
Net income							15,884.62			15,884.62
							535,692.00	535,692.00	319,880.00	319,880.00

WORKING PAPERS

Name _____

EXERCISE 12.1

GENERAL JOURNAL

PAGE _____

	DATE	DESCRIPTION	POST. REF.	DEBIT	CREDIT	
1						1
2						2
3						3
4						4
5						5
6						6
7						7

EXERCISE 12.2

_____

_____

_____

EXERCISE 12.3

GENERAL JOURNAL

PAGE _____

	DATE	DESCRIPTION	POST. REF.	DEBIT	CREDIT	
1						1
2						2
3						3
4						4
5						5
6						6
7						7
8						8
9						9
10						10
11						11
12						12
13						13
14						14
15						15
16						16
17						17
18						18

EXERCISE 12.4

GENERAL JOURNAL   PAGE _____

	DATE	DESCRIPTION	POST. REF.	DEBIT	CREDIT	
1						1
2						2
3						3
4						4
5						5
6						6
7						7
8						8
9						9
10						10
11						11
12						12
13						13

EXERCISE 12.5

GENERAL JOURNAL   PAGE _____

	DATE	DESCRIPTION	POST. REF.	DEBIT	CREDIT	
1						1
2						2
3						3
4						4
5						5
6						6
7						7
8						8

EXERCISE 12.6

GENERAL JOURNAL   PAGE _____

	DATE	DESCRIPTION	POST. REF.	DEBIT	CREDIT	
1						1
2						2
3						3
4						4

EXERCISE 12.7

GENERAL JOURNAL

	DATE	DESCRIPTION	POST. REF.	DEBIT	CREDIT	
1						1
2						2
3						3
4						4
5						5
6						6
7						7
8						8
9						9
10						10
11						11
12						12
13						13

PROBLEM 12.1A or 12.1B

GENERAL JOURNAL   PAGE _____

	DATE	DESCRIPTION	POST. REF.	DEBIT	CREDIT	
1						1
2						2
3						3
4						4
5						5
6						6
7						7
8						8
9						9
10						10
11						11
12						12
13						13
14						14
15						15
16						16
17						17
18						18
19						19
20						20
21						21
22						22
23						23
24						24
25						25
26						26
27						27
28						28
29						29
30						30
31						31
32						32
33						33
34						34
35						35
36						36
37						37

PROBLEM 12.1A or 12.1B (continued)

GENERAL JOURNAL

PAGE _____

	DATE	DESCRIPTION	POST. REF.	DEBIT	CREDIT	
1						1
2						2
3						3
4						4
5						5
6						6
7						7
8						8
9						9
10						10
11						11
12						12
13						13
14						14
15						15
16						16
17						17
18						18
19						19
20						20
21						21
22						22
23						23
24						24
25						25
26						26
27						27
28						28
29						29
30						30
31						31
32						32
33						33
34						34

Analyze: _____

_____

PROBLEM 12.2A or 12.2B

GENERAL JOURNAL   PAGE ____1____

	DATE		DESCRIPTION	POST. REF.	DEBIT	CREDIT	
1							1
2							2
3							3
4							4
5							5
6							6
7							7
8							8
9							9
10							10
11							11
12							12
13							13
14							14
15							15
16							16
17							17
18							18
19							19
20							20
21							21
22							22
23							23
24							24
25							25
26							26
27							27
28							28
29							29
30							30
31							31
32							32
33							33
34							34
35							35
36							36
37							37

PROBLEM 12.2A or 12.2B (continued)

GENERAL JOURNAL

PAGE ___2___

	DATE		DESCRIPTION	POST. REF.	DEBIT	CREDIT	
1							1
2							2
3							3
4							4
5							5
6							6
7							7
8							8
9							9
10							10
11							11
12							12
13							13
14							14
15							15
16							16
17							17
18							18
19							19
20							20
21							21
22							22
23							23
24							24
25							25
26							26
27							27
28							28
29							29
30							30
31							31
32							32
33							33
34							34

Analyze: _____

_____

PROBLEM 12.3A or 12.3B

	ACCOUNT NAME	TRIAL BALANCE		ADJUSTMENTS	
		DEBIT	CREDIT	DEBIT	CREDIT
1					
2					
3					
4					
5					
6					
7					
8					
9					
10					
11					
12					
13					
14					
15					
16					
17					
18					
19					
20					
21					
22					
23					
24					
25					
26					
27					
28					
29					
30					
31					
32					

PROBLEM 12.3A or 12.3B (continued)

_____

_____

ADJUSTED TRIAL BALANCE		INCOME STATEMENT		BALANCE SHEET		
DEBIT	CREDIT	DEBIT	CREDIT	DEBIT	CREDIT	
						1
						2
						3
						4
						5
						6
						7
						8
						9
						10
						11
						12
						13
						14
						15
						16
						17
						18
						19
						20
						21
						22
						23
						24
						25
						26
						27
						28
						29
						30
						31
						32

Analyze: _____

_____

PROBLEM 12.4A or 12.4B

	ACCOUNT NAME	TRIAL BALANCE		ADJUSTMENTS	
		DEBIT	CREDIT	DEBIT	CREDIT
1					
2					
3					
4					
5					
6					
7					
8					
9					
10					
11					
12					
13					
14					
15					
16					
17					
18					
19					
20					
21					
22					
23					
24					
25					
26					
27					
28					
29					
30					
31					
32					
33					
34					

PROBLEM 12.4A or 12.4B (continued)

ADJUSTED TRIAL BALANCE		INCOME STATEMENT		BALANCE SHEET		
DEBIT	CREDIT	DEBIT	CREDIT	DEBIT	CREDIT	
						1
						2
						3
						4
						5
						6
						7
						8
						9
						10
						11
						12
						13
						14
						15
						16
						17
						18
						19
						20
						21
						22
						23
						24
						25
						26
						27
						28
						29
						30
						31
						32
						33
						34

PROBLEM 12.4A or 12.4B (continued)

_____
_____

	ACCOUNT NAME	TRIAL BALANCE		ADJUSTMENTS	
		DEBIT	CREDIT	DEBIT	CREDIT
1					
2					
3					
4					
5					
6					
7					
8					
9					
10					
11					
12					
13					
14					
15					
16					
17					
18					
19					
20					
21					
22					
23					
24					
25					
26					
27					
28					
29					
30					
31					
32					

PROBLEM 12.4A or 12.4B (continued)

ADJUSTED TRIAL BALANCE		INCOME STATEMENT		BALANCE SHEET		
DEBIT	CREDIT	DEBIT	CREDIT	DEBIT	CREDIT	
						1
						2
						3
						4
						5
						6
						7
						8
						9
						10
						11
						12
						13
						14
						15
						16
						17
						18
						19
						20
						21
						22
						23
						24
						25
						26
						27
						28
						29
						30
						31
						32

Analyze: _____

PROBLEM 12.5A or 12.5B

_____

_____

_____

	ACCOUNT NAME	TRIAL BALANCE		ADJUSTMENTS	
		DEBIT	CREDIT	DEBIT	CREDIT
1					
2					
3					
4					
5					
6					
7					
8					
9					
10					
11					
12					
13					
14					
15					
16					
17					
18					
19					
20					
21					
22					
23					
24					
25					
26					
27					
28					
29					
30					
31					
32					
33					
34					

PROBLEM 12.5A or 12.5B (continued)

	ADJUSTED TRIAL BALANCE		INCOME STATEMENT		BALANCE SHEET		
	DEBIT	CREDIT	DEBIT	CREDIT	DEBIT	CREDIT	
							1
							2
							3
							4
							5
							6
							7
							8
							9
							10
							11
							12
							13
							14
							15
							16
							17
							18
							19
							20
							21
							22
							23
							24
							25
							26
							27
							28
							29
							30
							31
							32
							33
							34

PROBLEM 12.5A or 12.5B (continued)

	ACCOUNT NAME	TRIAL BALANCE		ADJUSTMENTS	
		DEBIT	CREDIT	DEBIT	CREDIT
1					
2					
3					
4					
5					
6					
7					
8					
9					
10					
11					
12					
13					
14					
15					
16					
17					
18					
19					
20					
21					
22					
23					
24					
25					
26					
27					
28					
29					
30					
31					
32					

PROBLEM 12.5A or 12.5B (continued)

_____

_____

	ADJUSTED TRIAL BALANCE		INCOME STATEMENT		BALANCE SHEET		
	DEBIT	CREDIT	DEBIT	CREDIT	DEBIT	CREDIT	
							1
							2
							3
							4
							5
							6
							7
							8
							9
							10
							11
							12
							13
							14
							15
							16
							17
							18
							19
							20
							21
							22
							23
							24
							25
							26
							27
							28
							29
							30
							31
							32

Analyze: _____

_____

PROBLEM 12.6A or 12.6B

	ACCOUNT NAME	TRIAL BALANCE		ADJUSTMENTS	
		DEBIT	CREDIT	DEBIT	CREDIT
1					
2					
3					
4					
5					
6					
7					
8					
9					
10					
11					
12					
13					
14					
15					
16					
17					
18					
19					
20					
21					
22					
23					
24					
25					
26					
27					
28					
29					
30					
31					
32					
33					
34					
35					

PROBLEM 12.6A or 12.6B (continued)

_____

_____

	ADJUSTED TRIAL BALANCE		INCOME STATEMENT		BALANCE SHEET		
	DEBIT	CREDIT	DEBIT	CREDIT	DEBIT	CREDIT	
							1
							2
							3
							4
							5
							6
							7
							8
							9
							10
							11
							12
							13
							14
							15
							16
							17
							18
							19
							20
							21
							22
							23
							24
							25
							26
							27
							28
							29
							30
							31
							32
							33
							34
							35

CRITICAL THINKING PROBLEM 12.1

	ACCOUNT NAME	TRIAL BALANCE		ADJUSTMENTS	
		DEBIT	CREDIT	DEBIT	CREDIT
1					
2					
3					
4					
5					
6					
7					
8					
9					
10					
11					
12					
13					
14					
15					
16					
17					
18					
19					
20					
21					
22					
23					
24					
25					
26					
27					
28					
29					
30					
31					
32					
33					

CRITICAL THINKING PROBLEM 12.1 (continued)

	ADJUSTED TRIAL BALANCE		INCOME STATEMENT		BALANCE SHEET		
	DEBIT	CREDIT	DEBIT	CREDIT	DEBIT	CREDIT	
							1
							2
							3
							4
							5
							6
							7
							8
							9
							10
							11
							12
							13
							14
							15
							16
							17
							18
							19
							20
							21
							22
							23
							24
							25
							26
							27
							28
							29
							30
							31
							32
							33

CRITICAL THINKING PROBLEM 12.1 (continued)

	ACCOUNT NAME	TRIAL BALANCE		ADJUSTMENTS	
		DEBIT	CREDIT	DEBIT	CREDIT
1					
2					
3					
4					
5					
6					
7					
8					
9					
10					
11					
12					
13					
14					
15					
16					
17					
18					
19					
20					
21					
22					
23					
24					
25					
26					
27					
28					
29					
30					
31					
32					

CRITICAL THINKING PROBLEM 12.1 (continued)

	ADJUSTED TRIAL BALANCE		INCOME STATEMENT		BALANCE SHEET		
	DEBIT	CREDIT	DEBIT	CREDIT	DEBIT	CREDIT	
							1
							2
							3
							4
							5
							6
							7
							8
							9
							10
							11
							12
							13
							14
							15
							16
							17
							18
							19
							20
							21
							22
							23
							24
							25
							26
							27
							28
							29
							30
							31
							32

CRITICAL THINKING PROBLEM 12.1 (continued)

GENERAL JOURNAL

	DATE	DESCRIPTION	POST. REF.	DEBIT	CREDIT	
1						1
2						2
3						3
4						4
5						5
6						6
7						7
8						8
9						9
10						10
11						11
12						12
13						13
14						14
15						15
16						16
17						17
18						18
19						19
20						20
21						21
22						22
23						23
24						24
25						25
26						26
27						27
28						28
29						29
30						30
31						31
32						32
33						33
34						34
35						35
36						36
37						37

CRITICAL THINKING PROBLEM 12.1 (continued)

GENERAL JOURNAL   PAGE ___32___

	DATE		DESCRIPTION	POST. REF.	DEBIT	CREDIT	
1							1
2							2
3							3
4							4
5							5
6							6
7							7
8							8
9							9
10							10
11							11
12							12
13							13
14							14
15							15
16							16
17							17
18							18
19							19
20							20
21							21
22							22
23							23
24							24
25							25
26							26
27							27
28							28
29							29
30							30
31							31
32							32
33							33
34							34
35							35
36							36
37							37

CRITICAL THINKING PROBLEM 12.1 (continued)

a. Net Sales _____

_____

_____

b. Net Delivered
Cost of Purchases _____

_____

_____

_____

_____

_____

c. Cost of Goods Sold _____

_____

_____

_____

_____

d. Net Income
(from worksheet) _____

_____

e. Capital,
December 31 _____

_____

_____

_____

Analyze: _____

_____

CRITICAL THINKING PROBLEM 12.2

1. _____
_____
_____
_____
_____

2. _____
_____
_____
_____
_____
_____
_____
_____
_____
_____
_____
_____
_____
_____
_____
_____
_____
_____
_____
_____
_____
_____

Chapter 12 Practice Test Answer Key

Part A True-False

1.	T	14.	T
2.	T	15.	F
3.	T	16.	F
4.	F	17.	F
5.	F	18.	T
6.	F	19.	T
7.	F	20.	F
8.	T	21.	T
9.	T	22.	T
10.	T	23.	F
11.	T	24.	T
12.	F	25.	T
13.	T		

Part B Exercises

GENERAL JOURNAL   PAGE 16

	DATE		DESCRIPTION	POST. REF.	DEBIT	CREDIT	
1			**Adjusting Entries**				1
2	2016		(Adjustment 1)				2
3	Dec.	31	Supplies Expense		1 4 0 0 00		3
4			Store Supplies			1 4 0 0 00	4
5			(Adjustment 2)				5
6		31	Interest Expense		2 5 00		6
7			Interest Payable			2 5 00	7
8			(Adjustment 3)				8
9		31	Interest Receivable		7 0 00		9
10			Interest Income			7 0 00	10
11			(Adjustment 4)				11
12		31	Insurance Expense		1 4 0 0 00		12
13			Prepaid Insurance			1 4 0 0 00	13
14							14
15			(Adjustment 5)				15
		31	Unearned Season Tickets Income		4 8 0 0 0 0 00		
			Season Tickets Income			4 8 0 0 0 0 00	

Financial Statements and Closing Procedures

STUDY GUIDE

Understanding the Chapter

Objectives

1. Prepare a classified income statement from the worksheet. **2.** Prepare a statement of owner's equity from the worksheet. **3.** Prepare a classified balance sheet from the worksheet. **4.** Journalize and post the adjusting entries. **5.** Journalize and post the closing entries. **6.** Prepare a postclosing trial balance. **7.** Journalize and post reversing entries. **8.** Define the accounting terms new to this chapter.

Reading Assignment

Read Chapter 13 in the textbook. Complete the textbook Section Self Review as you finish reading each section of the chapter, and the Comprehensive Self Review at the end of the chapter. Refer to the Chapter 13 Glossary or to the Glossary at the end of the book to find definitions for terms that are not familiar to you.

Activities

❏ **Thinking Critically**

Answer the *Thinking Critically* questions for Whole Foods Market and Managerial Implications.

❏ **Discussion Questions**

Answer each assigned discussion question in Chapter 13.

❏ **Exercises**

Complete each assigned exercise in Chapter 13. Use the forms provided in this SGWP. The objectives covered by an exercise are given after the exercise number. If you need help with an exercise, review the portion of the chapter related to the objective(s) covered.

❏ **Problems A/B**

Complete each assigned problem in Chapter 13. Use the forms provided in this SGWP. The objectives covered by a problem are given after the problem number. If you need help with a problem, review the portion of the chapter related to the objective(s) covered.

❏ **Critical Thinking Problems**

Complete the critical thinking problems as assigned. Use the forms provided in this SGWP.

❏ **Business Connections**

Complete the Business Connections activities as assigned to gain a deeper understanding of Chapter 13 concepts.

Practice Tests

Complete the Practice Tests, which cover the main points in your reading assignment. Compare your answers with those in the Practice Test Answer Key for Chapter 13 at the end of this chapter. If you have answered any questions incorrectly, review the related section of text.

Part A True-False

True-False For each of the following statements, circle T in the answer column if the statement is true or F if the statement is false.

T   F   1. A company reported net sales of $2,000,000 and cost of goods sold of $1,200,000. The gross profit percentage is 60%.

T   F   2. Some accounts adjusted in the Adjustment columns of the worksheet do not require a reversing entry.

T   F   3. Cash, accounts receivable, merchandise inventory, and equipment are classified as current assets.

T   F   4. **Interest Payable** and **Depreciation Expense** are typical of accounts that do not require reversing entries.

T   F   5. Reversing entries are not required, but are highly recommended in order to improve efficiency and reduce errors.

T   F   6. In closing the **Income Summary** account, the net income or loss is closed into the owner's capital account.

T   F   7. **Income Summary** is credited for the total of the expenses and the beginning inventory.

T   F   8. Closing journal entries for December 31, 2016 should be reversed on January 1, 2017.

T   F   9. The ending merchandise inventory is recorded in the accounting records by an adjusting entry.

T   F   10. Adjustments are posted from the worksheet to the general ledger accounts.

T   F   11. The depreciation expense for the store equipment appears in the Plant and Equipment section of the classified balance sheet.

T   F   12. The net income or loss from operations shown on the classified income statement is the difference between gross profit on sales and total operating expenses.

T   F   13. The Cost of Goods Sold section of the classified income statement includes information about the beginning and ending merchandise inventory and the purchases and net sales made during the year.

T   F   14. The gross profit on sales shown on the classified income statement is the difference between the net sales and the operating expenses.

T   F   15. Current liabilities are debts that are due for payment after one year from the balance sheet date.

T   F   16. Short-term notes receivable, cash, accounts receivable, merchandise inventory and prepaid expense items appear in the Current Assets section of the classified balance sheet.

T   F   17. The postclosing trial balance shows essentially the same account balances that appear in the balance sheet.

T   F   18. It is desirable to prepare a postclosing trial balance after the adjusting and closing entries have been journalized and posted.

T   F   19. The **Income Summary** account is closed at the end of the period.

T	F	**20.**	Asset, liability, and owner's capital accounts are the only accounts carried forward from one year to the next.
T	F	**21.**	The information needed to close the revenue and expense accounts is taken directly from the ledger accounts to ensure accuracy.
T	F	**22.**	The revenue and expense accounts are the only accounts carried forward from one year to the next.
T	F	**23.**	After completing the worksheet and the financial statements, adjustments are entered in the general journal.
T	F	**24.**	After all adjustments have been journalized and posted, the ledger account balances should be the same as the postclosing trial balance amounts.
T	F	**25.**	The drawing account is closed into the **Income Summary** account as one of the last closing entries.

Demonstration Problem

A partial worksheet showing the end-of-year operating results for Extreme Sports for 2016 follows.

Instructions

1. Prepare a classified income statement. Sports Warehouse does not classify its operating expenses as selling and administrative expenses.

2. Prepare a statement of owner's equity. No additional investments were made during the period.

3. Prepare a classified balance sheet as of December 31, 2016. All notes payable are due within one year.

4. Journalize the closing entries on page 45 of the general journal.

5. Compute the gross profit percentage for the year ended December 31, 2016. Round your answer to one decimal.

6. Compute the current ratio at December 31, 2016. Round your answer to two decimal places.

7. Compute the inventory turnover ratio for the year ended December 31, 2016. Round your answer to two decimal places.

8. Compute the accounts receivable turnover for the year ended December 31, 2016. The net accounts receivable balance at December 31, 2015 was $59,340. Round your answer to two decimal places.

DEMONSTRATION PROBLEM (continued)

Extreme Sports

Worksheet (Partial)

Year Ended December 31, 2016

	ACCOUNT NAME	INCOME STATEMENT DEBIT	INCOME STATEMENT CREDIT	BALANCE SHEET DEBIT	BALANCE SHEET CREDIT
1	Cash			25 285 00	
2	Accounts Receivable			61 258 00	
3	Allowance for Doubtful Accounts				5 930 00
4	Merchandise Inventory			197 214 00	
5	Supplies			3 512 00	
6	Prepaid Insurance			37 000 00	
7	Equipment			83 290 00	
8	Accumulated Depreciation—Equipment				24 330 00
9	Notes Payable				47 500 00
10	Accounts Payable				44 860 00
11	Social Security Tax Payable				2 683 00
12	Medicare Tax Payable				845 00
13	Salaries Payable				7 530 00
14	Interest Payable				3 660 00
15	Raul Flores, Capital				260 730 00
16	Raul Flores, Drawing			50 000 00	
17	Income Summary	201 345 00	197 214 00		
18	Sales		627 690 00		
19	Sales Returns and Allowances	11 950 00			
20	Purchases	280 174 00			
21	Purchases Returns and Allowances		10 440 00		
22	Freight In	11 410 00			
23	Purchases Discounts		11 921 00		
24	Telephone Expense	4 171 00			
25	Salaries Expense	241 380 00			
26	Payroll Tax Expense	13 104 00			
27	Supplies Expense	6 060 00			
28	Insurance Expense	5 000 00			
29	Depreciation Expense—Equipment	7 420 00			
30	Uncollectible Accounts Expense	2 600 00			
31	Interest Expense	3 160 00			
32	Totals	787 774 00	847 265 00	457 559 00	398 068 00
33	Net Income	59 491 00			59 491 00
34		847 265 00	847 265 00	457 559 00	457 559 00
35					

SOLUTION

(1.)

Extreme Sports

Income Statement

Year Ended December 31, 2016

Operating Revenue			
Sales			627 690 00
Less Sales Returns and Allowances			11 950 00
Net Sales			615 740 00
Cost of Goods Sold			
Merchandise Inventory, Jan. 1, 2016		201 345 00	
Purchases	280 174 00		
Freight In	11 410 00		
Delivered Cost of Purchases	291 584 00		
Less Purchase Returns and Allow.	10 440 00		
Purchase Discounts	11 921 00	22 361 00	
Net Delivered Cost of Purchases		269 223 00	
Total Merchandise Available for Sale		470 568 00	
Less Merchandise Inv., Dec. 31, 2016		197 214 00	
Cost of Goods Sold			273 354 00
Gross Profit on Sales			342 386 00
Operating Expenses			
Telephone Expense		4 171 00	
Salaries Expense		241 380 00	
Payroll Tax Expense		13 104 00	
Supplies Expense		6 060 00	
Insurance Expense		5 000 00	
Depreciation Expense—Equipment		7 420 00	
Uncollectible Accounts Expense		2 600 00	
Total Operating Expenses			279 735 00
Income from Operations			62 651 00
Other Expenses			
Interest Expense			3 160 00
Net Income for Year			59 491 00

SOLUTION (continued)

(2.)

Extreme Sports

Statement of Owner's Equity

Year Ended December 31, 2016

Raul Flores, Capital, Jan. 1, 2016			260 7 3 0 00
Net Income for Year	59 4 9 1 00		
Less Withdrawals for the Year	50 0 0 0 00		
Increase in Capital			9 4 9 1 00
Raul Flores, Capital, Dec. 31, 2016			270 2 2 1 00

(3.)

Extreme Sports

Balance Sheet

December 31, 2016

Assets			
Current Assets			
Cash			25 2 8 5 00
Accounts Receivable	61 2 5 8 00		
Less Allowance for Doubtful Accounts	5 9 3 0 00		55 3 2 8 00
Merchandise Inventory			197 2 1 4 00
Prepaid Expenses			
Supplies	3 5 1 2 00		
Prepaid Insurance	37 0 0 0 00		40 5 1 2 00
Total Current Assets			318 3 3 9 00
Plant and Equipment			
Equipment	83 2 9 0 00		
Less Accumulated Depreciation	24 3 3 0 00		
Total Plant and Equipment			58 9 6 0 00
Total Assets			377 2 9 9 00
Liabilities and Owner's Equity			
Current Liabilities			
Notes Payable	47 5 0 0 00		
Accounts Payable	44 8 6 0 00		
Interest Payable	3 6 6 0 00		
Social Security Tax Payable	2 6 8 3 00		
Medicare Tax Payable	8 4 5 00		
Salaries Payable	7 5 3 0 00		
Total Current Liabilities			107 0 7 8 00
Owner's Equity			
Raul Flores, Capital			270 2 2 1 00
Total Liabilities and Owner's Equity			377 2 9 9 00

SOLUTION (continued)

(4.)

GENERAL JOURNAL

PAGE ___45

	DATE		DESCRIPTION	POST. REF.	DEBIT	CREDIT	
1			**Closing Entries**				1
2	2016						2
3	Dec.	31	Sales		627 6 9 0 00		3
4			Purchase Returns and Allowances		10 4 4 0 00		4
5			Purchases Discounts		11 9 2 1 00		5
6			Income Summary			650 0 5 1 00	6
7							7
8		31	Income Summary		586 4 2 9 00		8
9			Sales Returns and Allowances			11 9 5 0 00	9
10			Purchases			280 1 7 4 00	10
11			Freight In			11 4 1 0 00	11
12			Telephone Expense			4 1 7 1 00	12
13			Salaries Expense			241 3 8 0 00	13
14			Payroll Taxes Expense			13 1 0 4 00	14
15			Supplies Expense			6 0 6 0 00	15
16			Insurance Expense			5 0 0 0 00	16
17			Depreciation Expense—Equipment			7 4 2 0 00	17
18			Uncollectible Accounts Expense			2 6 0 0 00	18
19			Interest Expense			3 1 6 0 00	19
20							20
21		31	Income Summary		59 4 9 1 00		21
22			Raul Flores, Capital			59 4 9 1 00	22
23							23
24		31	Raul Flores, Capital		50 0 0 0 00		24
25			Raul Flores, Drawing			50 0 0 0 00	25
26							26
27							27
28							28
29							29
30							30
31							31
32							32
33							33
34							34
35							35

(5.) The gross profit percentage for the year ended December 31, 2016 is 55.6% ($342,386/$615,740).

(6.) The current ratio at December 31, 2016 is 2.97 ($318,339/$107,078).

(7.) The inventory turnover ratio for the year ended December 31, 2016 is 1.37 ($273,354/$199,279.50).

(8.) The accounts receivable turnover ratio for the year ended December 31, 2016 is 10.74 ($615,740/$57,334).

WORKING PAPERS

EXERCISE 13.1

1. Purchases Returns and Allowances	_____
2. Telephone Expense	_____
3. Sales Returns and Allowances	_____
4. Purchases	_____
5. Interest Income	_____

6. Merchandise Inventory	_____
7. Interest Expense	_____
8. Sales	_____
9. Depreciation Expense— Store Equipment	_____
10. Rent Expense	_____

EXERCISE 13.2x

1. Accounts Receivable	_____
2. Delivery Van	_____
3. Prepaid Insurance	_____
4. Notes Payable, due 2014	_____
5. Store Supplies	_____

6. Accounts Payable	_____
7. Merchandise Inventory	_____
8. Ray Lynch, Capital	_____
9. Cash	_____
10. Unearned Subscription Income	_____

EXERCISE 13.3

(continued)

EXERCISE 13.3 (continued)

_____

_____

EXERCISE 13.4

_____

_____

EXERCISE 13.5

EXERCISE 13.6

GENERAL JOURNAL   PAGE _____

	DATE		DESCRIPTION	POST. REF.	DEBIT	CREDIT	
1							1
2							2
3							3
4							4
5							5
6							6
7							7
8							8
9							9
10							10
11							11
12							12
13							13
14							14
15							15
16							16
17							17
18							18
19							19
20							20
21							21
22							22
23							23
24							24
25							25
26							26
27							27
28							28
29							29
30							30
31							31
32							32
33							33
34							34
35							35
36							36
37							37

EXERCISE 13.7

GENERAL JOURNAL   PAGE _____

	DATE		DESCRIPTION	POST. REF.	DEBIT	CREDIT	
1							1
2							2
3							3
4							4
5							5
6							6
7							7
8							8
9							9
10							10
11							11
12							12
13							13
14							14
15							15
16							16
17							17
18							18
19							19
20							20
21							21
22							22
23							23
24							24
25							25
26							26
27							27
28							28
29							29
30							30
31							31
32							32
33							33
34							34
35							35
36							36
37							37

EXERCISE 13.8

ACCOUNT NAME	DEBIT	CREDIT

EXERCISE 13.9

a. Net Sales is

_____

_____

_____

Gross profit is

_____

_____

_____

The gross profit
percentage is

_____

_____

b. Current assets are

_____

_____

_____

_____

_____

_____

_____

_____

Current liabilities
are

_____

_____

_____

_____

_____

Working capital is

_____

_____

_____

_____

_____

_____

_____

_____

EXERCISE 13.9 (continued)

c. The current ratio is _____

_____

d. The inventory
turnover is _____

_____

_____

_____

_____

_____

_____

_____

_____

_____

_____

_____

_____

EXERCISE 13.10

a.

b.

PROBLEM 13.1A or 13.1B

(continued)

PROBLEM 13.1A or 13.1B (continued)

PROBLEM 13.1A or 13.1B (continued)

(continued)

PROBLEM 13.1A or 13.1B (continued)

Analyze: _____

PROBLEM 13.2A or 13.2B

(continued)

PROBLEM 13.2A or 13.2B (continued)

PROBLEM 13.2A or 13.2B (continued)

(continued)

PROBLEM 13.2A or 13.2B (continued)

Analyze: _____

_____

PROBLEM 13.3A or 13.3B

(continued)

PROBLEM 13.3A or 13.3B (continued)

PROBLEM 13.3A or 13.3B (continued)

(continued)

PROBLEM 13.3A or 13.3B (continued)

Analyze: _____

_____

PROBLEM 13.4A or 13.4B

GENERAL JOURNAL   PAGE _____

	DATE	DESCRIPTION	POST. REF.	DEBIT	CREDIT	
1						1
2						2
3						3
4						4
5						5
6						6
7						7
8						8
9						9
10						10
11						11
12						12
13						13
14						14
15						15
16						16
17						17
18						18
19						19
20						20
21						21
22						22
23						23
24						24
25						25
26						26
27						27
28						28
29						29
30						30
31						31
32						32
33						33
34						34
35						35
36						36
37						37

PROBLEM 13.4A or 13.4B (continued)

GENERAL JOURNAL

PAGE _____

	DATE		DESCRIPTION	POST. REF.	DEBIT	CREDIT	
1							1
2							2
3							3
4							4
5							5
6							6
7							7
8							8
9							9
10							10
11							11
12							12
13							13
14							14
15							15
16							16
17							17
18							18
19							19
20							20
21							21
22							22
23							23
24							24
25							25
26							26
27							27
28							28
29							29
30							30
31							31
32							32
33							33
34							34
35							35
36							36
37							37

PROBLEM 13.4A or 13.4B (continued)

GENERAL JOURNAL   PAGE _____

	DATE	DESCRIPTION	POST. REF.	DEBIT	CREDIT	
1						1
2						2
3						3
4						4
5						5
6						6
7						7
8						8
9						9
10						10
11						11
12						12
13						13
14						14
15						15
16						16
17						17
18						18
19						19
20						20
21						21
22						22
23						23
24						24
25						25
26						26
27						27
28						28
29						29
30						30
31						31
32						32
33						33
34						34
35						35
36						36
37						37

PROBLEM 13.4A or 13.4B (continued)

GENERAL JOURNAL

PAGE _____

	DATE		DESCRIPTION	POST. REF.	DEBIT	CREDIT	
1							1
2							2
3							3
4							4
5							5
6							6
7							7
8							8
9							9
10							10
11							11
12							12
13							13
14							14
15							15
16							16
17							17
18							18
19							19
20							20
21							21
22							22
23							23
24							24
25							25

Analyze: _____

_____

PAGE _____

	DATE		DESCRIPTION	POST. REF.	DEBIT	CREDIT	
1							1
2							2
3							3
4							4
5							5
6							6

PROBLEM 13.5A or 13.5B

PROBLEM 13.4A or 13.4B (continued)

GENERAL JOURNAL   PAGE _____

	DATE	DESCRIPTION	POST. REF.	DEBIT	CREDIT	
1						1
2						2
3						3
4						4
5						5
6						6
7						7
8						8
9						9
10						10
11						11
12						12
13						13
14						14
15						15
16						16
17						17
18						18
19						19
20						20
21						21
22						22
23						23
24						24
25						25
26						26
27						27
28						28
29						29
30						30
31						31
32						32
33						33
34						34
35						35
36						36

PROBLEM 13.5A or 13.5B (continued)

GENERAL JOURNAL   PAGE _____

	DATE		DESCRIPTION	POST. REF.	DEBIT	CREDIT	
1							1
2							2
3							3
4							4
5							5
6							6
7							7
8							8
9							9
10							10
11							11
12							12
13							13
14							14
15							15
16							16

Analyze: _____

_____

EXTRA FORM

GENERAL JOURNAL   PAGE _____

	DATE		DESCRIPTION	POST. REF.	DEBIT	CREDIT	
1							1
2							2
3							3
4							4
5							5
6							6
7							7
8							8
9							9
10							10
11							11
12							12
13							13

CRITICAL THINKING PROBLEM 13.1

	ACCOUNT NAME	TRIAL BALANCE		ADJUSTMENTS	
		DEBIT	CREDIT	DEBIT	CREDIT
1					
2					
3					
4					
5					
6					
7					
8					
9					
10					
11					
12					
13					
14					
15					
16					
17					
18					
19					
20					
21					
22					
23					
24					
25					
26					
27					
28					
29					
30					
31					
32					
33					
34					
35					
36					

CRITICAL THINKING PROBLEM 13.1 (continued)

	ADJUSTED TRIAL BALANCE		INCOME STATEMENT		BALANCE SHEET		
	DEBIT	CREDIT	DEBIT	CREDIT	DEBIT	CREDIT	
							1
							2
							3
							4
							5
							6
							7
							8
							9
							10
							11
							12
							13
							14
							15
							16
							17
							18
							19
							20
							21
							22
							23
							24
							25
							26
							27
							28
							29
							30
							31
							32
							33
							34
							35
							36

CRITICAL THINKING PROBLEM 13.1 (continued)

CRITICAL THINKING PROBLEM 13.1 (continued)

EXTRA FORM

CRITICAL THINKING PROBLEM 13.1 (continued)

CRITICAL THINKING PROBLEM 13.1 (continued)

GENERAL JOURNAL

PAGE _____

	DATE		DESCRIPTION	POST. REF.	DEBIT	CREDIT	
1							1
2							2
3							3
4							4
5							5
6							6
7							7
8							8
9							9
10							10
11							11
12							12
13							13
14							14
15							15
16							16
17							17
18							18
19							19
20							20
21							21
22							22
23							23
24							24
25							25
26							26
27							27
28							28
29							29
30							30
31							31
32							32
33							33
34							34
35							35
36							36
37							37

CRITICAL THINKING PROBLEM 13.1 (continued)

GENERAL JOURNAL

PAGE _____

	DATE	DESCRIPTION	POST. REF.	DEBIT	CREDIT	
1						1
2						2
3						3
4						4
5						5
6						6
7						7
8						8
9						9
10						10
11						11
12						12
13						13
14						14
15						15
16						16
17						17
18						18
19						19
20						20
21						21
22						22
23						23
24						24
25						25
26						26
27						27
28						28
29						29
30						30
31						31
32						32
33						33
34						34
35						35
36						36
37						37

CRITICAL THINKING PROBLEM 13.1 (continued)

GENERAL JOURNAL

PAGE _____

	DATE		DESCRIPTION	POST. REF.	DEBIT	CREDIT	
1							1
2							2
3							3
4							4
5							5
6							6
7							7
8							8
9							9
10							10
11							11
12							12
13							13
14							14
15							15
16							16
17							17
18							18
19							19
20							20
21							21
22							22
23							23
24							24
25							25
26							26
27							27
28							28
29							29
30							30
31							31
32							32
33							33
34							34
35							35
36							36
37							37

CRITICAL THINKING PROBLEM 13.1 (continued)

GENERAL JOURNAL   PAGE _____

DATE	DESCRIPTION	POST. REF.	DEBIT	CREDIT
1				
2				
3				
4				
5				
6				
7				
8				
9				
10				
11				
12				
13				
14				
15				
16				
17				
18				
19				
20				
21				
22				
23				
24				
25				
26				
27				
28				
29				
30				
31				
32				
33				
34				

Analyze: _____

_____

CRITICAL THINKING PROBLEM 13.2

1.

_____
_____

2. _____
_____
_____
_____
_____
_____

CHAPTER 13 CRITICAL THINKING PROBLEM (continued)

3.

Chapter 13 Practice Test Answer Key

Part A True-False

1. F	6. T	11. F	16. T	21. F
2. T	7. F	12. T	17. T	22. F
3. F	8. F	13. F	18. T	23. T
4. F	9. T	14. F	19. T	24. T
5. T	10. F	15. F	20. T	25. F

MINI-PRACTICE SET 2

Merchandising Business Accounting Cycle

SALES JOURNAL

PAGE _____

	DATE	SALES SLIP NO.	CUSTOMER'S NAME	POST. REF.	ACCOUNTS RECEIVABLE DEBIT	SALES TAX PAYABLE CREDIT	SALES CREDIT	
1								1
2								2
3								3
4								4
5								5
6								6
7								7
8								8
9								9
10								10
11								11
12								12
13								13
14								14

PURCHASES JOURNAL

PAGE _____

DATE	PURCHASED FROM	INVOICE NUMBER	INVOICE DATE	TERMS	POST. REF.	PURCHASES DR./ ACCOUNTS PAYABLE CREDIT

PAGE _____

CASH RECEIPTS JOURNAL

DATE	DESCRIPTION	POST. REF.	ACCOUNTS RECEIVABLE CREDIT	SALES TAX PAYABLE CREDIT	SALES CREDIT	OTHER ACCOUNTS CREDIT			CASH DEBIT
						ACCOUNT NAME	POST. REF.	AMOUNT	

CASH PAYMENTS JOURNAL

PAGE _____

DATE	CK. NO.	DESCRIPTION	POST. REF.	ACCOUNTS PAYABLE DEBIT	OTHER ACCOUNTS DEBIT			PURCHASES DISCOUNTS CREDIT	CASH CREDIT
					ACCOUNT NAME	POST. REF.	AMOUNT		

Name _____

GENERAL JOURNAL   PAGE _____

	DATE		DESCRIPTION	POST. REF.	DEBIT	CREDIT	
1							1
2							2
3							3
4							4
5							5
6							6
7							7
8							8
9							9
10							10
11							11
12							12
13							13
14							14
15							15
16							16
17							17
18							18
19							19
20							20
21							21
22							22
23							23
24							24
25							25
26							26
27							27
28							28
29							29
30							30
31							31
32							32
33							33
34							34
35							35
36							36
37							37
38							38

GENERAL JOURNAL

	DATE		DESCRIPTION	POST. REF.	DEBIT	CREDIT	
1							1
2							2
3							3
4							4
5							5
6							6
7							7
8							8
9							9
10							10
11							11
12							12
13							13
14							14
15							15
16							16
17							17
18							18
19							19
20							20
21							21
22							22
23							23
24							24
25							25
26							26
27							27
28							28
29							29
30							30
31							31
32							32
33							33
34							34
35							35
36							36
37							37
38							38

Name _____

GENERAL JOURNAL

PAGE _____

	DATE		DESCRIPTION	POST. REF.	DEBIT	CREDIT	
1							1
2							2
3							3
4							4
5							5
6							6
7							7
8							8
9							9
10							10
11							11
12							12
13							13
14							14
15							15
16							16
17							17
18							18
19							19
20							20
21							21
22							22
23							23
24							24
25							25
26							26
27							27
28							28
29							29
30							30
31							31
32							32
33							33
34							34
35							35
36							36
37							37
38							38

GENERAL LEDGER

ACCOUNT _____ ACCOUNT NO. _____

DATE		DESCRIPTION	POST. REF.	DEBIT	CREDIT	BALANCE	
						DEBIT	CREDIT

ACCOUNT _____ ACCOUNT NO. _____

DATE		DESCRIPTION	POST. REF.	DEBIT	CREDIT	BALANCE	
						DEBIT	CREDIT

ACCOUNT _____ ACCOUNT NO. _____

DATE		DESCRIPTION	POST. REF.	DEBIT	CREDIT	BALANCE	
						DEBIT	CREDIT

ACCOUNT _____ ACCOUNT NO. _____

DATE		DESCRIPTION	POST. REF.	DEBIT	CREDIT	BALANCE	
						DEBIT	CREDIT

Name _____

GENERAL LEDGER

ACCOUNT _____ ACCOUNT NO. _____

DATE	DESCRIPTION	POST. REF.	DEBIT	CREDIT	BALANCE	
					DEBIT	CREDIT

ACCOUNT _____ ACCOUNT NO. _____

DATE	DESCRIPTION	POST. REF.	DEBIT	CREDIT	BALANCE	
					DEBIT	CREDIT

ACCOUNT _____ ACCOUNT NO. _____

DATE	DESCRIPTION	POST. REF.	DEBIT	CREDIT	BALANCE	
					DEBIT	CREDIT

ACCOUNT _____ ACCOUNT NO. _____

DATE	DESCRIPTION	POST. REF.	DEBIT	CREDIT	BALANCE	
					DEBIT	CREDIT

ACCOUNT _____ ACCOUNT NO. _____

DATE	DESCRIPTION	POST. REF.	DEBIT	CREDIT	BALANCE	
					DEBIT	CREDIT

Name _____

GENERAL LEDGER

ACCOUNT _____ ACCOUNT NO. _____

DATE		DESCRIPTION	POST. REF.	DEBIT	CREDIT	BALANCE	
						DEBIT	CREDIT

ACCOUNT _____ ACCOUNT NO. _____

DATE		DESCRIPTION	POST. REF.	DEBIT	CREDIT	BALANCE	
						DEBIT	CREDIT

ACCOUNT _____ ACCOUNT NO. _____

DATE		DESCRIPTION	POST. REF.	DEBIT	CREDIT	BALANCE	
						DEBIT	CREDIT

ACCOUNT _____ ACCOUNT NO. _____

DATE		DESCRIPTION	POST. REF.	DEBIT	CREDIT	BALANCE	
						DEBIT	CREDIT

Name _____

GENERAL LEDGER

ACCOUNT _____ ACCOUNT NO. _____

DATE	DESCRIPTION	POST. REF.	DEBIT	CREDIT	BALANCE	
					DEBIT	CREDIT

ACCOUNT _____ ACCOUNT NO. _____

DATE	DESCRIPTION	POST. REF.	DEBIT	CREDIT	BALANCE	
					DEBIT	CREDIT

ACCOUNT _____ ACCOUNT NO. _____

DATE	DESCRIPTION	POST. REF.	DEBIT	CREDIT	BALANCE	
					DEBIT	CREDIT

ACCOUNT _____ ACCOUNT NO. _____

DATE	DESCRIPTION	POST. REF.	DEBIT	CREDIT	BALANCE	
					DEBIT	CREDIT

ACCOUNT _____ ACCOUNT NO. _____

DATE	DESCRIPTION	POST. REF.	DEBIT	CREDIT	BALANCE	
					DEBIT	CREDIT

GENERAL LEDGER

ACCOUNT _____ ACCOUNT NO. _____

DATE		DESCRIPTION	POST. REF.	DEBIT	CREDIT	BALANCE	
						DEBIT	CREDIT

ACCOUNT _____ ACCOUNT NO. _____

DATE		DESCRIPTION	POST. REF.	DEBIT	CREDIT	BALANCE	
						DEBIT	CREDIT

ACCOUNT _____ ACCOUNT NO. _____

DATE		DESCRIPTION	POST. REF.	DEBIT	CREDIT	BALANCE	
						DEBIT	CREDIT

ACCOUNT _____ ACCOUNT NO. _____

DATE		DESCRIPTION	POST. REF.	DEBIT	CREDIT	BALANCE	
						DEBIT	CREDIT

GENERAL LEDGER

ACCOUNT _____ ACCOUNT NO. _____

DATE	DESCRIPTION	POST. REF.	DEBIT	CREDIT	BALANCE DEBIT	BALANCE CREDIT

ACCOUNT _____ ACCOUNT NO. _____

DATE	DESCRIPTION	POST. REF.	DEBIT	CREDIT	BALANCE DEBIT	BALANCE CREDIT

ACCOUNT _____ ACCOUNT NO. _____

DATE	DESCRIPTION	POST. REF.	DEBIT	CREDIT	BALANCE DEBIT	BALANCE CREDIT

ACCOUNT _____ ACCOUNT NO. _____

DATE	DESCRIPTION	POST. REF.	DEBIT	CREDIT	BALANCE DEBIT	BALANCE CREDIT

ACCOUNT _____ ACCOUNT NO. _____

DATE	DESCRIPTION	POST. REF.	DEBIT	CREDIT	BALANCE DEBIT	BALANCE CREDIT

GENERAL LEDGER

ACCOUNT _____ ACCOUNT NO. _____

DATE	DESCRIPTION	POST. REF.	DEBIT	CREDIT	BALANCE	
					DEBIT	CREDIT

ACCOUNT _____ ACCOUNT NO. _____

DATE	DESCRIPTION	POST. REF.	DEBIT	CREDIT	BALANCE	
					DEBIT	CREDIT

ACCOUNT _____ ACCOUNT NO. _____

DATE	DESCRIPTION	POST. REF.	DEBIT	CREDIT	BALANCE	
					DEBIT	CREDIT

ACCOUNT _____ ACCOUNT NO. _____

DATE	DESCRIPTION	POST. REF.	DEBIT	CREDIT	BALANCE	
					DEBIT	CREDIT

ACCOUNT _____ ACCOUNT NO. _____

DATE	DESCRIPTION	POST. REF.	DEBIT	CREDIT	BALANCE	
					DEBIT	CREDIT

Name _____

GENERAL LEDGER

ACCOUNT _____ ACCOUNT NO. _____

	DATE	DESCRIPTION	POST. REF.	DEBIT	CREDIT	BALANCE	
						DEBIT	CREDIT

ACCOUNT _____ ACCOUNT NO. _____

	DATE	DESCRIPTION	POST. REF.	DEBIT	CREDIT	BALANCE	
						DEBIT	CREDIT

ACCOUNT _____ ACCOUNT NO. _____

	DATE	DESCRIPTION	POST. REF.	DEBIT	CREDIT	BALANCE	
						DEBIT	CREDIT

ACCOUNT _____ ACCOUNT NO. _____

	DATE	DESCRIPTION	POST. REF.	DEBIT	CREDIT	BALANCE	
						DEBIT	CREDIT

ACCOUNT _____ ACCOUNT NO. _____

	DATE	DESCRIPTION	POST. REF.	DEBIT	CREDIT	BALANCE	
						DEBIT	CREDIT

ACCOUNTS RECEIVABLE SUBSIDIARY LEDGER

NAME _____ TERMS _____

	DATE	DESCRIPTION	POST. REF.	DEBIT	CREDIT	BALANCE

NAME _____ TERMS _____

	DATE	DESCRIPTION	POST. REF.	DEBIT	CREDIT	BALANCE

NAME _____ TERMS _____

	DATE	DESCRIPTION	POST. REF.	DEBIT	CREDIT	BALANCE

NAME _____ TERMS _____

	DATE	DESCRIPTION	POST. REF.	DEBIT	CREDIT	BALANCE

NAME _____ TERMS _____

	DATE	DESCRIPTION	POST. REF.	DEBIT	CREDIT	BALANCE

ACCOUNTS RECEIVABLE SUBSIDIARY LEDGER

NAME _____ TERMS _____

DATE	DESCRIPTION	POST. REF.	DEBIT	CREDIT	BALANCE

NAME _____ TERMS _____

DATE	DESCRIPTION	POST. REF.	DEBIT	CREDIT	BALANCE

ACCOUNTS PAYABLE SUBSIDIARY LEDGER

NAME _____ TERMS _____

DATE	DESCRIPTION	POST. REF.	DEBIT	CREDIT	BALANCE

NAME _____ TERMS _____

DATE	DESCRIPTION	POST. REF.	DEBIT	CREDIT	BALANCE

ACCOUNTS PAYABLE SUBSIDIARY LEDGER

NAME _____   TERMS _____

DATE	DESCRIPTION	POST. REF.	DEBIT	CREDIT	BALANCE

	ACCOUNT NAME	TRIAL BALANCE		ADJUSTMENTS	
		DEBIT	CREDIT	DEBIT	CREDIT
1					
2					
3					
4					
5					
6					
7					
8					
9					
10					
11					
12					
13					
14					
15					
16					
17					
18					
19					
20					
21					
22					
23					
24					
25					
26					
27					
28					
29					
30					
31					
32					
33					
34					
35					
36					

ADJUSTED TRIAL BALANCE		INCOME STATEMENT		BALANCE SHEET		
DEBIT	CREDIT	DEBIT	CREDIT	DEBIT	CREDIT	
						1
						2
						3
						4
						5
						6
						7
						8
						9
						10
						11
						12
						13
						14
						15
						16
						17
						18
						19
						20
						21
						22
						23
						24
						25
						26
						27
						28
						29
						30
						31
						32
						33
						34
						35
						36

Name _____

_____

_____

	ACCOUNT NAME	TRIAL BALANCE		ADJUSTMENTS	
		DEBIT	CREDIT	DEBIT	CREDIT
1					
2					
3					
4					
5					
6					
7					
8					
9					
10					
11					
12					
13					
14					
15					
16					
17					
18					
19					
20					
21					
22					
23					
24					
25					
26					
27					
28					
29					
30					
31					
32					
33					
34					
35					
36					

_____
_____

	ADJUSTED TRIAL BALANCE		INCOME STATEMENT		BALANCE SHEET		
	DEBIT	CREDIT	DEBIT	CREDIT	DEBIT	CREDIT	
							1
							2
							3
							4
							5
							6
							7
							8
							9
							10
							11
							12
							13
							14
							15
							16
							17
							18
							19
							20
							21
							22
							23
							24
							25
							26
							27
							28
							29
							30
							31
							32
							33
							34
							35
							36

Name _____

_____

_____

Name _____

ACCOUNT NAME	DEBIT	CREDIT

EXTRA FORMS

_____

_____

	ACCOUNT NAME	TRIAL BALANCE		ADJUSTMENTS	
		DEBIT	CREDIT	DEBIT	CREDIT
1					
2					
3					
4					
5					
6					
7					
8					
9					
10					
11					
12					
13					
14					
15					
16					
17					
18					
19					
20					
21					
22					
23					
24					
25					
26					
27					
28					
29					
30					
31					
32					
33					
34					

ADJUSTED TRIAL BALANCE		INCOME STATEMENT		BALANCE SHEET		
DEBIT	CREDIT	DEBIT	CREDIT	DEBIT	CREDIT	
						1
						2
						3
						4
						5
						6
						7
						8
						9
						10
						11
						12
						13
						14
						15
						16
						17
						18
						19
						20
						21
						22
						23
						24
						25
						26
						27
						28
						29
						30
						31
						32
						33
						34

Name _____

EXTRA FORM

GENERAL JOURNAL   PAGE _____

	DATE		DESCRIPTION	POST. REF.	DEBIT	CREDIT	
1							1
2							2
3							3
4							4
5							5
6							6
7							7
8							8
9							9
10							10
11							11
12							12
13							13
14							14
15							15
16							16
17							17
18							18
19							19
20							20
21							21
22							22
23							23
24							24
25							25
26							26
27							27
28							28
29							29
30							30
31							31
32							32
33							33
34							34
35							35
36							36
37							37